MW01225264

To Know Å Fallen Angel

by

Bernard Amador

authorHOUSE™

1663 LIBERTY DRIVE, SUITE 200
BLOOMINGTON, INDIANA 47403
(800) 839-8640
WWW.AUTHORHOUSE.COM

First published by AuthorHouse 09/23/04

ISBN: 1-4184-9822-X (sc)

Library of Congress Control Number: 2004096899

Printed in the United States of America
Bloomington, Indiana

This book is printed on acid-free paper.

Even though this is a true story and the author has endeavored to be accurate, the names of people and places have been changed.

" And the fifth angel blew his trumpet, and I saw a star that had fallen from heaven to earth. "

Revelations 9:1

For

Johnny
Bunny
And
Bill

Table of Contents

What's In A Name?

Ma	Mother
Pa	Father
Michael	Who is like God
Douglas	Dark
Levi	He who unites
Catherine	Purity
Christopher	Bearer of Christ
Gabriel	Man of God
Eva	Life
Hannah	Grace
Uriel	Light of God
Ruth	Companion
Benjamin	Son of the right hand
Melissa	Bee
Flora	Flower
Jerome	Holy name
Andrew	Manly
Jason	Healer
Patrick	Aristocrat
Colin	Dove
Rachelle	Lamb
Rochelle	Stone
Roxana	Dawn of Day
Theresa	She who reaps
Lyle	Of the Island
Angela	Messenger
Jennifer	One who loves peace
Cathy	Pure
Robert	One with bright fame
Ari	Lion
Joseph	God will increase

Prologue

To Know À Fallen Angel is the true coming of age story of how a young boy tries not to become a sexual predator. Michael is a child who grows up in the heart of the poverty stricken South Bronx in an apartment filled with sexual abuse, and incest fueled by alcoholism and domestic violence. As the story unfolds, the sexual abuse Michael experiences results in a misunderstanding between father and son that separates them emotionally and leaves the boy with a desire to know what it would be like to have a "normal" relationship with his father. It also leads to the development of sexual predatory behaviors in Michael.

Michael escapes from the abusive household by using school as a refuge to protect him, and manages to preserve a balanced morality until the abuse becomes overwhelming and penetrates him physically and mentally. Michael tries to create a barrier in his mind between himself and the abuse but instead he experiences a mental breakdown. As he grows older, Michael embarks on a quest to understand his abuser and his developing self. Motivated by the desire to know the roots of his sexual abuse, Michael uses genealogical therapy to trace the events of his youth. Along the way he discovers a typology of the sexual predator, and identifies different types of sexual predators by classifying their methods, motivation and victimology.

By identifying the type of predator that abused him, Michael discovers how he himself developed sexual predatory behaviors and ultimately understands how the mind of one type of sexual predator functions. With the identification of the root source of his sexual abuse, the motivations behind it and the victimology, the specific type of sexual predator is caught in the nominological net. By understanding what has prevented him from perpetuating the same abuse on others Michael discovers possible treatment methods for the sexual predator, one of the most difficult criminals to treat. In the end Michael triumphs over his abuse, the urge to perpetuate it, and reconciles with his father to develop a relationship that was once lost.

Chapter I:
The Desire to Know

It was like a whisper that lands upon one's eardrum but instead it was softly pressing against my lower back. I lay on the bed in my Fruit of the Looms with the white elastic and the fine blue stripe; as the pressing got stronger and stronger, I felt myself gain consciousness from a deep sleep gasping for air. As I opened my eyes I could feel a final thrust and a warm liquid substance land on my back. The room was cooled by the gentle wind blowing past the sound of fluttering curtains hanging from the open window near the bed.

There were arms above my shoulders and the smell of sweat wafting past my face turned to the side, as I lay there still and stiff. Oh so gently did a soft fabric wipe the warm liquid off my back and I see a cotton T-shirt drop out of a hand on to the floor beside the bed. The activity caused my body to tremble for I did not understand what was happening. The lace curtained French doors of the den were open before me as I lifted my head. A radio advertisement for Bold laundry detergent came from another room in the apartment and faded as a figure disappeared through the doors taking my innocence with it.

As I pushed upwards on my hands, I saw a Miller High Life sign displayed across the top shelf above the French doors. In front of the sign was an old rotating ironing machine. I rose from the single bed and moved closer to the doors, slowly turning the knob of the French door and entering the living room, afraid of what might be in the next room. The figure was not there and as I passed through the living room and entered the hallway, the memory ends.

This is the earliest memory I have of it. My desire to know about the event was developing, but I did not know at the time what it all meant. When I recall the memory I feel like I am dreaming. Remembering my childhood physically puts me in a dream state, a condition therapists call dissociation. Sometimes the memories are triggered by the least little thing and return to me in a flash when I least expect them. When they do, it feels like a revelation that helps me understand my life.

The memories usually take me back to the year 1973, when I developed a fascination for what was between my father's legs. I had learned at an early age that my father had something between his legs I wanted to see, to touch, and to know. Little did I realize the desire to know would be pressed upon my mind for years to come. Where my dream-like memory ends, my conscious memory fills in the blanks.

Every morning as a child I took the same route, out of the French doors through the living room past my parent's bedroom on the way to the kitchen. There my mother sat sipping her morning coffee. When she spotted me the morning routine began.

"Good morning," she said to me daily.

"Good morning, Ma," I'd say as she took my hand and led me into the bathroom next door.

The cold bathroom tiles made the lower part of my body shiver and woke me up while my face was in the mist of steam from the bath my father had just taken. She reached above the sink, and pulled out my blue toothbrush from the rest of the bunch hanging in the rack and handed it to me. As I held my toothbrush she squeezed about a fourth of an inch of toothpaste on it and instructed me to brush.

"Don't forget to brush your tongue," she said as she turned around and headed back into the kitchen to finish her coffee.

When I returned to the kitchen she had a bowl of corn flakes waiting for me on the table. On warm days she had cold cereal for me to eat. On cold days she prepared a hot bowl of oatmeal or cornmeal. Yellow cornmeal was my favorite. After breakfast my mother led me back down the hallway to the living room where she sat me down in front of the television and put on my favorite shows. Mornings for the first five years of my life were spent in front of the television and running around the seven-room apartment while my older brothers and sisters were already out of the apartment attending school.

As I sat watching the screen, my mother passed by often going in and out of every bedroom doing housework. The beds were the first things she tackled, and then she searched through large laundry bags to separate the colors from the whites. If the sheets on the bed were dirty, they became part of the daily laundry to be washed. Load after load she washed. After washing she took the wet clothes in a large bundle and set them out to dry. The apartment had a clothes line that extended from my older sisters Uriel and Ruth's bedroom window, at the end of the apartment near

3

the front door, to my parents' bedroom window. The clothes line passed Hannah's window, the bathroom window, and kitchen window before it reached my parents' bedroom.

Hannah was the oldest sister living with us. She acted just like Ma and always kept behind the rest of the children in the family to make sure we were doing the right thing and not getting into any trouble. She was the role model for the girls in the family and set the example by doing well in school. Hannah helped get the girls ready for school in the morning by brushing their hair or consulting with Ma about which outfit her sisters were to wear for the day. She was being reared to be a true matriarch.

Hannah physically looked like a matriarch, strong with a heavy build. Her strong, rough edge was framed by soft white skin and long ash brown hair that flowed down her face over her shoulders and past her buttocks. Her soft speech contrasted her frame, but her words were as intelligent and strong as the time she spent learning them. She was a conformist and was being molded to have a traditional family life ruled by a matriarch.

Uriel on the other hand was a rebel. The darkness of her skin and hair gave her a shield of strength. She too had long hair that flowed past her buttocks but it was thick and strong like her attitude. It was obvious that she began to act out the moment she realized there was something different about her and Ruth, who were a few days apart in age. Uriel was told at a young age that her sister Ruth was adopted. Ma brought Ruth and Uriel home at the same time from the hospital. Ruth was abandoned by her biological parents. A day before Ma was about to leave the hospital with Uriel, the midwife caring for her entered her hospital room.

"Do you think you can care for another child?" the midwife asked.

"I have to talk to my husband, " Ma replied.

The day Ma left the hospital she brought home two girls instead of one. Like Uriel, Ruth had a dark complexion and short coarse dark hair that grew around her head like a nimbus. Ruth was a curious girl who tried to make herself fit into a family she was told at a young age she was not genetically part of. This knowledge created a division between Uriel and Ruth and started a battleground for what was rightfully theirs. Uriel did what she was told to do, but not without a fight and she constantly made Ruth's life a living hell.

Uriel was very independent and when anyone tried to help her she made it difficult for them. By adopting Ruth my parents sent a message to Uriel that she was not special, so during her childhood she became a tomboy, hanging out with my older brother Benjamin and his friends and getting into trouble. Ruth tried to prove she belonged to Ma by following closely in Hannah's footsteps. Like Hannah she always followed the younger children to make sure they were doing the right thing.

Uriel on the other hand spent a lot of time alone or talking with me. She was instrumental in showing me the ropes about what was expected from me since she also spent time with my brother Benjamin and his friends. Uriel and I became very close and I knew a side of her that she only let me see.

The windows in my sisters' room faced the back of the apartment building into the alley, while the den with the French doors I slept in with my brothers Benjamin and younger brother Jerome faced the side of the building. Benjamin was three years older than me and was very aggressive. He was tall with dark black hair and brown eyes.

Though he was tall he appeared chunky, not being able to get rid of his baby fat.

Benjamin was the oldest brother living with us, like Hannah, and set the example for the boys. When he came home from school, he quickly finished his homework and went directly to Ma.

"Can I go with Pa?" he asked.

"No, you father is busy," Ma answered.

"Then can I go next door?" he asked.

"It's dinner time, wait till later," Ma would say. It was always the same routine with Benjamin.

As Jerome grew he followed in Benjamin's footsteps. He wanted to be just like Benjamin, although instead of going outside he wanted to watch cartoons and learn about the new toys that were being advertised on television. Jerome was shy. He was a fair-skinned red headed boy with freckles. Jerome was not my brother, but like Ruth he was adopted into the family.

Technically Jerome was my nephew, the son of my oldest sister Catherine. Catherine became pregnant while in the military. In those days pregnant girls who did not marry the father of their child were sent away, or the baby was given up for adoption. Ma would not allow Catherine to give Jerome up for adoption but instead raised him as her own.

Having Jerome in the family gave me a fuller understanding of what Uriel felt the day she learned Ruth was adopted, because I was given a similar explanation about Jerome. I was able to understand and see the tension between my older two sisters and what I had to look forward to.

Out of the living room windows across the street one could see Public School 21. The school was like a huge

6

fortress built in Gothic style with gargoyles watching over the courtyard where the children played during recess. The left view from the windows encompassed a portion of Trinity Avenue. From five floors above one could see Gill's grocery store and the social club my father frequented. To the right, on an angle, one could see Pete's store on the corner, the schoolyard to Public School 144 down the hill, and Intermediate School 161 across the street from it. Only portions of these buildings could be seen because the fire escape obstructing the right view. Near the window with the fire escape sat the television.

On schedule my mother approached the television set and turned the knob to change the channel-no channel surfing with a remote in those days. As one show ended she was quick enough to put on another. After watching *David and Goliath, Puss and Boots,* and *Sesame Street*, it was time for lunch and then my afternoon nap. Ma stopped her chores to prepare a peanut butter and jelly sandwich, baloney and cheese, or a bowl of soup for my lunch.

"Michael," Ma called.

"Yes, Ma," I yelled.

When I heard my name I jumped up and ran down the hallway into the kitchen where my lunch was waiting for me. The kitchen table was against the wall under a row of three shelves. On each shelve sat a row of clear drinking glasses. The centerpiece of the glass layout was a brown jug that had a porcelain nude woman stuck in the nozzle by a cork that extended from her rear end. The woman's breasts had two holes where the nipples should have been that held two toothpicks, the kind with the frilly ends. There she sat with her legs crossed and a smile on her face. Below her read, "Keep your hands off the old man's bundle." Under the shelves was a picture of my grandmother.

The picture of Ma's mother was wrapped in clear plastic and taped to the wall over the table, resembling a shrine. My grandmother died in 1968, the year I was born. When she passed on, my mother could not believe she was gone and banged her head against the wall. It was the women who held the family together and kept it going. The line of tradition was becoming weak with the passing of my grandmother. Those lessons that only a grandmother taught were now in the hands of Ma. Grandma was from a family who stole horses for a living in Europe and did what she had to inorder to survive. Grandma came to the United States for a better life in the late twenties but was faced with the Great Depression and had to struggle to survive.

Survival in the 1960's was likewise a harsh reality for Ma with eight young children, a dying mother and expecting me at any moment. It was apparent as time passed my mother had difficulty dealing with the loss of her mother. She knew she had to go on, that there were too many children to give up on. Having already placed five children from previous relationships in an orphanage and starting over, she was not about to give up on her children again. But while Ma spent her day taking care of the children, her evenings were filled with binge drinking to escape the reality of her mother's death. A mother of nine, she was soon a mother of thirteen.

Ma went through the same routine with all thirteen of us, cooking and cleaning day in and day out. It appeared she had fallen behind on her work. As I sat at the table eating my sandwich, I could feel the spinning of the washing machine. It was past noon and all of the laundry was not done.

"Are you finished?" she asked as she popped into the kitchen to check on me.

"All done," I said as she wiped my face and hands and instructed me to take a nap.

Some mornings when I was up, Pa would be sleeping from a late night at the social club. Other mornings he was up early and showered, having coffee and warm Italian bread with butter at the kitchen table while I ate my cereal. By noon Pa was out of the house and I was put to bed in the den for a peaceful afternoon nap.

One Saturday afternoon after my nap, I took the same path through the apartment as I did the morning of my earliest memory. From my bedroom I walked out the French doors and through the living room to the hallway. After a few steps I took a right into the door of my parents' bedroom where Pa was sleeping. I knew it was he because I could smell Glover's in the room. My father was losing his hair and he thought the anti-dandruff product would stimulate his hair growth.

The smell became stronger as I quietly approached the bed. He was lying there as he always did, with a sheet over his head blocking the sunlight stretching across the bed from the adjacent window. My curiosity was stronger than the scent of Glovers; I wanted to know, to understand what it was. As I got closer to the bed I placed my hand under the cover near my father's foot dangling off the side of the bed and stretched it up my father's legs. He must have felt my arm making its way up his leg and jumped up from his deep sleep screaming.

"Hey, what are you doing?" he yelled. When he saw me standing beside the edge of the bed he began to scream.

"Hey, get this boy out of here."

Before I could blink, Ruth ran into the bedroom and pulled me from the bed.

"Come on Michael," she said, and dragged me out of the room into the long hallway.

"Ruth, what is wrong with your father?" Ma asked. We entered the kitchen and Ruth explained, "Ma, Pa is trying to sleep and Michael was waking him up."

My sister did not witness the full event, so she gave my mother an account based on what she saw.

"When I went in the room I saw Michael standing in from of Pa near the bed," she said.

Standing in front of my mother, as Ruth explained the event, Ma turned to me.

"Do not wake your father when he is sleeping," she scolded. "Now go inside and watch TV."

When Ma finished scolding me, I was let go and went about my daily activities. I also began to constantly think about the event.

Since that afternoon, I got the feeling that my relationship with Pa was no longer the same. As I grew older I tried to understand what possessed me to go in my parents' room that day. That single event changed the course of my history with my father. That night Pa left the apartment but I did not see him leave. He returned late that night and left early the next morning. We did not get to have breakfast together like we usually did. I did not get to see Pa until a full day later. When I did finally get to see Pa, he acted like he did not want to see me. My father no longer looked me in the face. His behavior made me feel as if I should no longer look at him. The level of communication changed between us.

"Tell that boy to go and get my shoes," he'd instruct Ma.

Pa no longer talked directly to me. If he wanted to tell me something or give me something to do, he looked at Ma and gave her the information to pass on to me.

"Tell that boy to put my slippers in the room," he'd say as I stood before him.

I was being punished like Adam and Eve after they ate from the tree of knowledge of good and evil. As part of their punishment God distanced himself from them, and my father began a process of distancing himself from me. The shame and fear that developed as a result did not decrease my desire to know what was between his legs. This knowledge unfortunately was learned elsewhere.

At age 5, I did not understand the difference between right and wrong involved in this event. It was when I became older that the difference became clear to me. I did, however, learn the value of money at a very young age. Pa gave us all a weekly allowance. I remember getting fifty cents a week. There was so much I could buy with that amount. Bazooka gum only cost one cent and was a great deal. Not only did you get a whopping piece of gum that could be divided into two pieces, but the package also included a mini cartoon of Blondie and Dagwood, which was my favorite. Ruth used to call me Blondie because I had natural blond highlights.

On special days when I bought the gum I got a tattoo instead of a cartoon. The tattoos were most likely to be included in the summer months. Having the power to spend seemed to be a nice thing as a child, especially knowing that if I had money, I could get candy for it or almost whatever I wanted. When I had money, it was comforting. Most of the time I was without it. My allowance was spent before the weekend was out. Pa gave Ma our allowance to distribute on Friday nights when he got home from the club. My cut was fifty cents which I was given on Saturday mornings.

Since my money went so quickly on candy, I took any opportunity to make additional change. At the age of five I developed a hustler's mentality. My sisters, brothers and I were allowed in the social club when my father and his friends were gambling, so perhaps I inherited my father's ways through modeling. When I was out of change during the week I helped my father as he worked on the family car or washed it. All I had to do was stand by him and Benjamin and he ordered my brother to instruct me to get a particular tool from the trunk of the car.

"Tell that boy to get me the wrench," he said to Benjamin.

"Michael, get Pa the wrench," Benjamin instructed.

"This one," I yelled holding up the pliers.

"No, the other one, its orange," Benjamin yelled at me as I searched the toolbox in the trunk of the car.

As I searched for the tool I wondered what the tool was like between my fathers' legs. Pa continued to communicate to me by his actions that I was not to speak directly to him, but the time spent with Pa was cherished, since it was the only true quality time I could spend with him as I got older. The days of having breakfast with him at the same table were over.

Things were not going too well for me. Not only did Pa distance himself from me but I was soon sent off to kindergarten. The time helping Pa also was cherished mainly because it gave me the opportunity to make some extra change, but it was not the only opportunity I had to make money. If I helped around the apartment, Ma tried her best to give me anything I wanted.

"If I had it, I would give it to you," Ma said.

She always knew when we wanted something. It seemed to be a mother's instinct, but I later learned that a child approaches adults in a slow and cautious way with eyes facing upwards, showing fear and a strong curiosity. As time went on I realized it was a relationship with my father that I wanted.

* * * *

But I also wanted money so Uriel or Benjamin could take me to the store to buy candy. When Pa was not around there were other ways of making money. Having so many brothers and sisters, the opportunities to make money for favors abounded. I even had the opportunity to make money-playing games with my half brother Douglas. Douglas always had a game for me to play. As a child I did not have the cognition for higher reasoning that would make me question or understand why a child in a family of 13 children had to pay someone money to play with him.

Many times I was led into the dark hallway of the apartment building by Douglas to play a game that I thought could get me some money. The hallway was painted brown and white with dull florescent lighting. The floor had octagon marble tiles that formed a mosaic pattern. Most of the time the hall windows were left open to air out the stench of dry urine from the neighbors' dog that was let out to urinate but stopped short and urinated in the hallway.

Little did I know I would pay a price more valuable than the few pieces of change I was promised for playing the silly game. The only way to describe the game is by calling it the endless pocket. In order to be led to the hallway, I first was tricked into doing something like carry a pair of shoes into the bedroom for a few cents. This was an easy task because Pa always had us carry his slippers to the bedroom in the morning for him as he put his boots on while sitting at the kitchen table.

"If you want your money come with me into the hallway," Douglas said.

In order for me to get the change, I had to go into the hallway to retrieve my earnings. Stepping over a puddle of dry dog urine, it did not occur to me at the time that I was being set up to play the game while I was in the apartment. In order for me to get my earnings I had to get the money myself from an endless pocket.

"Here is your money," Douglas said with his hand in his pocket.

I could hear a few coins rattle between his fingers. Like magic I went in to retrieve the money I was promised but it was not there. I called this the endless pocket game because not only was the money gone when I reached down into the pocket to get it, but the bottom of the pocket was cut out. When I reached for what I earned, I searched through an endless pocket and got something else.

"No, don't take your hand out, hold on to it," Douglas instructed.

As I held on I felt warm flesh grow in my hand. After a while my finding pulsed and became moist at the top.

"It's getting wet," I said.

"Hold on, don't let go," he said.

This stimulated my curiosity. When a neighbor entered the hall or came up the stairs Douglas quickly pulled away.

"Be quiet," he said.

I'd let go and he did not give me any money. When the coast was clear the game began again.

"If you want your money, put your hand in and get it," he told me.

The game was an endless trap. When I did not get the money, the stakes were raised.

"Try again, I'll give you fifty cents," he said.

The reward would increase, not understanding how it was that when he placed his hand in the pocket the sound of change would rattle around and when it was my turn the money was gone. At the time I did not understand what he was doing. I can remember the game going on for a while until I gave up. It was good that Douglas did not know the dynamics of classical conditioning, for if he rewarded me with some of my earnings I'm sure I would have continued to play as long as he wanted me to.

The game ended when I was left holding a hard pulsing, slippery object that discontinued growing, with no monetary reward. He was very clever in his method of preying on my innocence. In the end I never got the money I was promised. I now understand the desire, and know where my curiosity began, in trying to understand what was between my father's legs.

Chapter II:
Method to the Madness

Ma married at a young age and gave birth to Catherine, Christopher and Gabriel. After this marriage failed she got involved with a man and became pregnant with Eva, one of my older sisters. After the birth of Eva, Ma no longer took take care of her four children and became involved with the court system for drug use and neglect. The court gave her the option of going to jail for drug use or a treatment facility. She decided to be placed in the House of the Good Shepherd, in Peekskill, New York. The House of the Good Shepherd is a not-for-profit corporation that today still provides families with treatment, education and support services that hopefully have a positive and lasting impact on their ability to function individually, as a family and in the community.

The best option Ma had for Catherine, Christopher, Gabriel and Eva, was to place them in Mount Loretta, an orphanage on Staten Island for children who had no place to go. Of the four, Catherine, Christopher and Gabriel never really visited Ma while they were young and spent the early years of their life at Mount Loretta–so I really never got to know them back then. When Ma returned from the House of the Good Shepherd, she became involved with yet another man and became pregnant, this time with Douglas. She was not able to take care of him either and placed him in the Catholic orphanage St. Joseph's By The Sea at Huguenot, Staten Island, an annex to the New York Foundling Hospital for orphaned infants that opened in 1910. By the time Ma placed Douglas at St Joseph's, a social service department had been established in order to provide case worker services for unmarried mothers.

St. Joseph's By The Sea is where Douglas grew up and I believed learned the methods of a sexual predator. After Ma met and developed a relationship with Pa, and had four more children, Douglas was a teen who had mastered a method of sexual abuse. He often came to our apartment to visit or stay with us and preyed on Hannah, Uriel, Benjamin, Ruth, Flora, Melissa, Jerome, and me. My mind began recording the abuse as early as 1973 in our 5th floor apartment in a building on Jackson Avenue in the South Bronx. Douglas was very mechanical and seemed to lack emotion when he abused me. The early recordings my mind made of him taught me he had a methodology of abuse I too learned.

In 1973 I was sent off to kindergarten. The first day Ma brought me to school I cried and cried. We left our building on Jackson Avenue and headed towards the school across the street. At 158th Street we walked a block to Trinity Avenue. I could see my den window in the distance as we tuned the corner and headed for the main entrance of the school. As we entered the building through the large brown metal doors on Trinity Avenue, I saw the gargoyles looking down at me. Ma led me by the hand.

"Come on, Michael, hurry or we'll be late, " she said to me.

"I'm coming Ma," I said.

We headed down a long hallway with bulletin boards and large colorful signs that read "Welcome Back," held up by thumbtacks. To the left was a door with a line of parents outside it. Above the door a sign read "Administration Office." Ma brought me there first to find out what class I was assigned to. When it was our turn she showed the woman behind the counter a letter in a yellow envelope.

"My son is scheduled to start school today," Ma told the lady.

"Did you bring his immunization card?" the lady behind the desk asked.

"Yes, all his paper work is in the envelope," Ma replied. The woman directed us.

"Second floor, room 201, Ms. Green is the teacher," the woman behind the desk told my mother.

"Thank you," my mother replied.

"This way, Michael, to the second floor," Ma said as she led me by the hand.

The staircase leading to the second floor was directly across from the Administration Office. The up and down stairs were separated by a smoky glass. As Ma and I climbed the stairs to the second floor we saw the shadows of other people descending through the glass. When we got to the second floor we passed through a brown swinging door and on the right was my new classroom. The perimeter of the room was filled with toys of all kinds.

In the center of the room were desks and chairs for the students while the teacher's desk was in front of the black board in front of the room.

"Good morning, this is my son Michael," Ma said.

"Good morning, I'm Ms. Green," said the tall skinny lady wearing a bright lime green dress that was as perky as her greeting. Ms. Green eagerly took my hand from Ma's and directed me to my assigned seat.

"Michael, I have to go now. Uriel will bring you home later today," said Ma.

"Are you leaving so soon?" asked Ms. Green.

"Yes, I have much house work to do," Ma said, letting Ms. Green know that she too was a career woman.

As Ma left I ran to the door and started to cry. Ms. Green ran ahead of me and shut the door. I was too short to reach the glass window of the door to watch Ma as she disappeared down the hall.

Ms. Green left me by the door as I continued to cry. By the time I stopped crying and turned away from the door the classroom was filled with other children and it was lunch time. Lunch was brought up to our classroom by lunch room aids. Ms. Green tried to get me to eat. All the other children quickly ate up the spaghetti on their plates and drank their milk. Watching them, I began to get hungry. Ma never made me spaghetti for lunch, I thought. Ms. Green noticed that I sat down at my assigned seat where my lunch was waiting for me. After eating she tried to get my attention by directing the other children and myself to a playground outside the back door of the classroom.

"Come on children, it's playtime!" Ms. Green called.

The playground was built on top of the first floor lunch room and its entrance was from my classroom. Our classroom was the only room that led to the playground on the top of the school lunch room and was enclosed in a steel gate to which Ms. Green took the children after we ate our lunch. Wanting to go out with the other children, I quickly washed my hands and face and headed for the open door to the playground.

Little animals, a rocket and a hopscotch board were painted in pastel colors on the floor of the roof. The painted figures included a train and a track that spread throughout the floor of the cage. Ms. Green pointed out the design of the train and each of its cars and explained their functions, from the engine car to the caboose. I thought our play was symbolic for the message she was trying to impress on our psyche. The teacher encouraged the children to form a line on the railroad track and make believe we were a train by marching along the track.

"Choo choo! Chug-a-chug-a, Choo choo!," she shouted for us to repeat.

Just as Ma's rotating ironing machine in my earliest memory, the functionalist idea of a mechanical man, or man as machine, was pressed upon and circling around in our little minds so we saw ourselves in this way. It was early training to function like machines and become society's worker bees as adults. This was a remnant of the industrial revolution of which Karl Marx would have approved.

Seeing right through her little exercise, I declined to participate and separated myself from the group of little lambs that were being led to slaughter. The following year, stories surfaced and I listened as Ma read a specific *Time* magazine article titled, *Marvel of the Bronx, Robot Teaching Fourth Graders* that told of students in the South Bronx who were learning from robots that acted as models for them to mimic. From the time we entered kindergarten we were to think of mechanisms and how they run so we would eventually behave as them.

As I grew older I was able to see how my perception of reality began in that steel-gated playground on the roof. Standing in the corner of the playground, I also could see the window of the living room to our apartment. Seeing our

21

window made me cry because I wanted to be home with Ma. How I longed to be at home in front of the television eating a peanut butter and jelly sandwich watching *Puss & Boots* like I use to do every day. Instead, I was in a cage with a bunch of strange children I did now know. Soon it was time to go home and Uriel was standing at the classroom door to pick me up.

"Uriel dear, please remind your mother that Michael has a doctor's appointment this week," Ms. Green told Uriel.

"Yes, I will let her know," Uriel said.

A few days after I entered school, I was called to the nurse's office for a check up. My entrance checkup with the school doctor was scheduled in the afternoon close to leaving time. After my examination, Ma was very fortunate that Child Protection Services was not called. All the new students were called to the doctor's office to get a measles shot. On the day of my examination, I remember the doctor opening up my pants and feeling my stomach. His hand moved below my navel to the right.

"Does it hurt here?" the doctor asked. He moved his hand to the left.

"No," I answered.

"How about here?" he asked. He then pressed even harder in the center.

"No."

"Does it hurt here?" he asked.

"No."

This form of examination felt familiar to me. As his hand went lower below my navel in my pants I became aroused. The doctor quickly stopped his examination and helped me zipper up my pants. Uriel was waiting outside the doctor's office to pick me up and take me home. I left his office with an erection and my zipper partially down. As

I left the school building on my way home, I cried. Uriel tried grabbing my hand but I purposefully walked behind her. I did not want her to see my erection or my crying. Uriel turned around.

"What's wrong Michael?" she asked.

"Nothing, leave me alone," I said

"Hurry up, Michael, I want to get home to eat," she said.

As I walked behind her I passed the fire hydrant in the middle of the block and hit it with my school knapsack. I did not understand why this was happening to me at home and now it was happening to me at school, somewhere I did not want to be in the first place.

The doctor who gave me the check up at school could have notified the authorities and explained to them that a child was exhibiting sexual behavior at such an early age. Later I learned and grew to believe it is normal for a young baby to get an erection when a diaper is changed, but at five years old, sexual arousal is a red flag if it is achieved without intention and it indicates that sexual abuse may be occurring. In my case the authorities should have been notified. The doctor did not think it was important enough to notify my parents or Child Protective Services.

Today I understand that there were no systems in place at the time for detecting child abuse or laws for mandated reporting. The 1974 Supreme Court case *Tarasoff v Regents* that brought mandated reporting to the forefront did not commence until one year after my experience with the school doctor. When the day of my checkup came, and the doctor opened my pants, I misunderstood him checking me and took it for him wanting to play with me like Douglas did at home.

That event really made me feel like I did not want to be in school. The days I spent in school were eventful but I would rather have been at home with Ma. Miraculously there were many different events that kept me out of school. One event was head lice. The thought of having little bugs crawling on my scalp crept me out but the reward of staying home from school quickly helped me get over it. Those insects had a field day living on my scalp since my hair was very thick and curly.

If any one of us had lice, all of us had to go through the process of being rid of them. Ma would line us up outside the bathroom with our own individual towel and one by one call us in. First was the application of a thick and smelly shampoo that burned but was effective in killing the lice. Next she rapped our heads up in a torn tee shirt and allowed the shampoo to soak in for about a half an hour. My sisters always went first since they had beautiful long hair.

Watching the process made me cringe, especially the next step. After rinsing the scalp, Ma sectioned the hair and took a fine toothcomb to it. Watching my younger sister cry as my mother pulled the comb through her hair sent chills up my spine.

"Ma, that hurts," Uriel screamed as my mother continued to part the hair and pull the comb through it.

"Please, Ma, stop!" Uriel cried.

My sister looked as if she was being tortured, flinching as my mother pulled. Unfortunately, I was next. The process was not as bad as it looked. The fine tooth comb did not hurt a bit. I was more freaked out by Ma pressing her fingernail along the side of the comb to kill the lice.

"Crack! Crack! Snap!," is all one heard as her fingernail went across the side of the comb; the bugs were cracking and snapping under her fingernail. It is possible the lice were not caught from children in school but from Douglas who visited often from the orphanage. He most likely caught them from his abuser, who I now imagine frequented infested porno theaters and passed them on to us. Regardless of where they came from, having lice allowed me to stay home from school.

Another thing that kept me out of school was chicken pox. Having the chicken pox was not as easy as having lice. It took longer to get rid of them and the experience was even less pleasant. One after the other my sisters and brothers lined up outside the bathroom to take a bath. After we dried off Ma applied Calamine lotion to our whole bodies to prevent our skin from itching.

It was extremely painful if we scratched open a pox, Ma then applied alcohol directly to the open pox.

"Ouch Ma, that burns," I screamed.

"Stay still, will you?" she said as she poured more alcohol onto a cotton ball and applied it to the next area of skin with poxes that had been scratched at.

That is exactly what happened to me when I scratched open a pox under my right arm. My brother Benjamin and I also had a pox on the same exact spot on our faces that opened and left scars around our left eye. The pain was so strong that I dreamt I obtained the scars by falling in the courtyard of P.S. 21 while running away from the school. I dreamed I was transferred to the hospital after the fall and a microchip was implanted in my frontal lobe above my eye where the scar was. The microchip was planted to test if a new technology worked with young children who disobeyed the orders of authority.

My lack of obedience to authority was known the day I refused to follow Ms. Green's instructions to act mechanical in the school yard, and differentiated me from

25

the other children in school. This history behind my dream made me feel estranged from my classmates. While I was home from school with the chicken pox, my teacher sent a gift and a small basket of candy home with Uriel. The gift was wrapped in red tissue paper with a blue yarn bow tie. I quickly opened it up to find a book that told the story of a little boy "Blue" who blew his horn and when he was being looked for fell fast asleep under a haystack. These gifts made me miss the class, but I did not want to return to school.

The ambivalence that developed in me about attending school was resolved the day a classmate named Levi helped clarify the confusions I was experiencing. Every afternoon after playtime Ms. Green took the girls and boys down the hall in a double line to the bathroom. One afternoon I had to go to the bathroom and my penis began to get erect because I was holding my urine. Levi saw my erect penis and was fascinated by it. While I urinated he came over and grabbed and pulled at it.

The first time it happened my body trembled. My breath was rapid and there was terror in my body as my heart started to beat quickly and the sweat poured from underneath my arms. There was a big smile on Levi's face and I started to understand that he was getting pleasure from the experience. From that day on it was difficult going to the bathroom in school. This time there was no mistake, this event I was experiencing was identical to what I was experiencing at home with Douglas.

The next few days in school when the class lined up to go to the bathroom after playtime, Levi lined up behind me so that we'd go into the bathroom together. Levi taunted me.

"Come on man, let me see it!"

"Stop it!" I said.

"Let me play with it," he continued.

"I'm telling Ms. Green," I threatened, hoping he'd leave me alone.

I physically fought to get him away from me. It was an annoyance for me but I saw the pleasure he was getting by the widening of his big blue eyes and dilating pupils. My encounters with Levi helped me understand. By now I put two and two together and realized the dynamics of the pocket game that Douglas played with me. Was it pleasure I was supposed to get from the game, I asked myself? I was learning quickly how I was to react in Levi's wide eyes. So, this is what the pocket game was all about. Being placed in the role of my older brother, I saw myself in Levi, searching, grabbing, pulling, and tugging.

A powerful sense of revelation came over me. In the place of innocence stood fear. Where there was fear it was now pleasure. Where there was pleasure there was knowledge and a newfound realization. The system of events was imbedded into my core. The desire to know grew stronger. From then on I wanted to learn more and filled my life with seeking and acquiring knowledge.

My interaction with Levi made me realize what the thing between my father's legs was all about. In my newfound understanding I discovered a non-physical part of me. I was beyond what Sigmund Freud called the phallic stage that focuses on physical pleasure. It was a realization that Michel Foucault would later write about when he wrote of bio-power, the use of pleasure and care of the self in his *History of Sexuality Volumes I-III.* Sexuality was now a part of my existence.

Sexuality and the behavior needed to experience the pleasure that it brought was further associated with a spiritual world I explored on Sundays when my older sister Hannah took me to St. Anselm's Church. Having sexuality and the pleasure it brought at such a young age led me to believe there was something more to life than the icons with angelic tones displayed in the church. Praying to gain a greater understanding of it all, God was giving me the answers one at a time. The situation at home with Douglas was identical to the sexual play at school with Levi.

Douglas's method was to attack in the middle of the night or early in the morning when everyone was still sleeping so he would not get caught. He was a pro at it because my parents never found out. My brother became so good in his methodology that his skills were beginning to be utilized during the daytime when my mother was occupied with company and sitting at the kitchen table having a cup of coffee.

"Come on, Michael, Ma has company," Douglas said.

"Thank you, Douglas," Ma said.

"Let's go inside and play," Douglas said as I followed him down the hall into the den where I slept.

There he took me into the room and closed the French doors and began one of his games. Sophisticated, he devised the little games to feed on my innocence. Levi on the other hand was an amateur. The virus of sexual abuse must have made itself known to him, though he seemed more knowledgeable than I was, or were we just two children innocently exploring each other's bodies? Levi did not care if the other boys saw what he was doing-he was careless. He was not afraid of the possibility of being caught by an authority as Douglas was.

Levi never got caught and I learned how to avoid him. My avoidance led him to move on to other boys in the class. Ms. Green never checked on us while we were in the bathroom, even when it seemed that we were taking a very long time. The other boys in the class, who new of Levi, quickly used the urinals and ran out of the bathroom when they saw him come in. Whenever Levi approached me, I wished I could get out easily, but Levi was a bully. He did not let me leave until he was finished fondling me.

Douglas was similar in that he continued to abuse me until he was satisfied or I woke up during the incident and made it known to him that I was up. Douglas then stopped until I fell asleep again or he thought I was asleep, then he crept up to my bed, mounted me and began his dry humping till he reached an orgasm. He was like a charged machine that did not stop until his power source ran out.

When Levi learned he could no longer get satisfaction from me after playtime in the bathroom, he stopped seeking me out and moved on to other boys. The other boys began to talk to one another and to the teacher about Levi. Ms. Green finally questioned him. The other boys never told Ms. Green what Levi did with me.

The boys explained the incidents as Levi attempting to bother them while they were trying to use the bathroom. My classmates left out the sexual nature of the events in their explanation. What was non-sexual for the other boys in my class was sexual for me. By Levi's reaction it was obviously sexual for him. We both gained a knowledge the other children seemed not to have really understood. I am grateful these events were as short lived as my attendance at P.S. 21.

The chicken pox and lice kept me out of school that year and made the school year go by much quicker. My stay at P.S. 21 was brief since the school closed down while I was in first grade. Before the school closed Hannah had the chance to graduate, while Uriel, Benjamin, Ruth, Flora,

Melissa, Jerome, and me were transferred to Public School 144. The closing down of P.S. 21 happened when Douglas seemed to have shut down, as his visits to my bed at night became less frequent.

Chapter III:
Developing a System

Douglas visited on and off during our transition from P. S. 21 to P. S. 144; his methodology unknowingly was being experienced by all the children in the apartment and developed into a system. The system was able to flourish as a result of our individual silence. By remaining silent Douglas was able to go from one child to the next like a bee feeding on several flowers. Through this pollination he was polluting our minds with knowledge unsuitable for children. The lessons I learned compelled me to search for answers to the bigger questions in life like: Does God exist? If so, why was he allowing me to be abused? I also wondered whether people were machines.

These were not questions that could get answered at home, so I looked to school for the answers and an escape from the abuse. The knowledge learned at home mainly involved issues of domestic violence, how to be an absent father, alcoholism, and most importantly sexual abuse and incest that fed the system and allowed it to develop.

In retrospect I believe my mother did her best for someone with one failed marriage and many children. She ran the household like a boot camp, with ten of us in the apartment. Ma collected her welfare check, paid the bills, and bought the basic necessities with whatever was left. Although she constantly told us that she loved us, it was said so often that it seemed to lack true emotional value. But I know she did love us. Individually she took Hannah, Uriel, Benjamin, Ruth, Flora, Melissa, Jerome, and me and carved out special time for each of us. My time was in the evening before bedtime.

"Time for bed," Ma yelled from her bedroom.

She was already in bed, indicating to me that it was my time to spend with her alone.

"I don't want to go to bed yet, Ma," I said standing in her doorway while all the other children headed for their rooms.

"OK, come lay here with me," she said.

Each night Douglas stayed over it was the same routine. Ma held me as I lay in front of her on the edge of the bed. It was a very nurturing experience for me. Little did she know that she was protecting me during that time. This was more nurturing than I received from my father. Turning the knob of the television, she would search for something appropriate for us to watch. I knew when it was late in the evening and I was about to be sent to my room. At the same time every night I was in bed with her a scary show began. Airy music played as a hand came up from the ground and a deep voice screeched, "Chilleeeeeeeeerrr." Boy did that scare the hell out of me. By then it was time to return to the bedroom I shared with my brothers.

"Time to go to bed," she said.

It was unfortunate that she did not know what happened in the den two doors away. For a woman who was abused as a child herself, she apparently did not pick up the clues

I tried to give her about the sexual abuse. She did not see why I always asked to stay with her on the nights Douglas was over. How I wanted to tell her what was going on when Douglas stayed over but I was afraid of a spanking and punishment.

Besides, Ma had her own problems. She felt that her problems made her unworthy of love. One way this showed was that she always played a record titled, *Oh Johnny*. Years before, the song was meant as a warning to my father from his friends not to marry her or else there would be problems. The song went:

> His name is Johnny, as we all know,
> And I married Bunny cause I loved her so.
> Oh Johnny we told you not to marry.
> Yes we told you not to marry Bunny.
> You were so young and so was she.
> Now you went and got yourself a family.
> Now you' re going to see what you' re going through
> ...Oh I miss those friends of mine.
> I haven't seen them in a long long time.
> I want to see them so I can bail in the snow,
> But Bunny wants to follow everywhere I go.
> If I go out Bunny has a fit,
> So I have to stay home and baby-sit.
> Oh Johnny we told you not to marry.
> Yes we told you not to marry Bunny.

Pa never did marry her until the children were grown. Ma continued to be a very heavy drinker and smoker after the death of her mother. The refrigerator always had bottles of Miller High Life in it and the nightstand near her bed was full of cartons of Winchesters cigars-she preferred

33

cigars over cigarettes. These problems did not compare to the fact that my father came home early around the time she received the welfare check and beat her like a jockey beat a horse in the final stretch of a race.

To me it appeared that this happened every night. Most of the time it was over money. Pa would lose his money betting on the horses or in a card game and wanted my mother to take from her welfare check to finance his habit. Not only did he beat Ma, but also he destroyed the furniture, especially if it was new. I did not understand why he did such things. This was the main reason why I was terrified at the idea of telling Pa what was going on when Douglas was around, in addition to searching between his legs when I was five. I don't think he ever had a clue either about Douglas, partly because he was never around.

Since he was always with his friends trying to make ends meet gambling, Pa spent most of his days and nights at a social club and came home around two or three in the morning, just after Douglas was finished abusing one of us. I also believe Pa did the best he could with what he had. My father did not have an education to help him get a good paying job.

Ma financed his existence or he made money running the numbers or playing them and the horses. From my perspective it seemed like he loved the horses more than he loved me. He blew the money he made back on gambling in card games with his friends, on the numbers or playing the horses.

Going to the racetrack seemed like the only time he spent with the family. He took us to Aqueduct, Belmont or Saratoga during the warm months. There he took us to the horse's circle where we viewed the horses before he placed his bets. Children present were allowed to pet the horses. I watched Pa as he pat the horses three times on their collar as they circled hoping it brought his horse in first place.

If he made extra money and felt like taking us away, we went on longer trips. One year he took us to Niagara Falls. Another year we all went to Washington, D.C. But we never visited the Caribbean as children. Pa was raised on a Caribbean island and sent to the United States as a young man to help raise money to support his family. His one true love was to watch the horses run in the field and he dreamt about being a jockey. Instead of following his dream he was forced to travel to the U.S. to work.

As we got older the trips got shorter. We took trips in the evening to Coney Island, or to Orchard Beach in the Bronx and stayed till the next morning. These were happy times for me. We had Pa to ourselves without any of his friends around. But his network of friends in the community was often beneficial to the family. There were always other people in addition to Hannah, looking out for us and giving my father a report when Uriel, Benjamin, Ruth, Flora, Melissa, Jerome, or I got in trouble.

Strangely, when it came to disciplining the children, Pa was a passive man who rarely hit us, but when he did it was hard. Ma really wore the pants in the family, though I will never forget the first beating I received from my father. Benjamin and I loved to play skullzies with our friends during the summer months. We drew boxes in the middle of the street with chalk, hating it when we were interrupted as cars passed by and rolled over our skullzies' tops. If the top was made of a plastic soda cap filled with clay, asphalt or melted crayon, it got squished by the weight of the car.

The best tops were made out of metal and taken from the bottom of school chairs. Those particular tops had to be taken off the chairs with pliers when the teacher was not looking. The metal bottom scrapped across the cement sidewalk caused the metal top to glide. To prevent the tops from gliding too far, the black rubber interior was scrapped out of the top and filled with the filling of one's choice.

Most players filled their tops with melted crayons. Crayola produced so many different colored crayons that everyone who played individualized their top by color. There was a whole process involved in filling a top. First, one needed a top, crayons, a candle and matches. The crayon is then broken into pieces and placed in the metal top. The top is held over a burning candle to melt the crayon wax. Then the top was set aside to cool. If the top was not metal one had to hold the crayon above the top and hold a lit match or lighter against it to melt the crayon into the top.

My crayon of choice was aqua blue. This was the color that I chose to fill my top with Benjamin one night. We had our supplies ready and waited until everyone was asleep. Ma and Pa did not allow Benjamin and I to play with matches at our age, so we waited until everyone was asleep. This was something I learned from Douglas. If you wanted to get away with something, you should do it at night while everyone was asleep.

The punishment for such behavior was to take our hand and place it over the flames of the burning gas stove in the kitchen. Getting caught for smoking was twice as bad. If one of us was caught smoking, Ma made him light up a cigar in front of her. She then made him inhale a long puff of the cigar smoke, then drink a large glass of water right after it was inhaled.

Swallowing smoke and water can make anyone choke. I choked the day I toyed with Ma about wanting to smoke. After one long puff of her Winchesters and the glass of water to follow, the desire to smoke left me for good. Nor did I have the urge to play with matches because after getting punished for smoking, she placed my hands over the flame on the stove for playing with matches to light the cigar.

But I had the desire to play with matches the night Benjamin and I filled our tops. With everyone asleep we took an old box with our supplies inside and started to light matches under the old French Provincial marble table in the corner of the den. As we worked on filling the tops in the den the box caught fire.

"Put it out," I said as Benjamin tried to put the fire out. I ran to the den window.

"Throw the box out the window. Hurray up," I said as I opened the window.

Benjamin lifted the box from under the marble table and headed toward the window. The curtains on the French doors caught fire. An armoire that held Hannah's wardrobe with lace curtains on the doors also went up in flames.

We could not throw the box out the window, since the window only opened up as far as the top of the protective gates. The curtains on the window also caught fire.

"Benjamin throw the box out of the living room window," I said as I ran down the hallway to get a pot of water from the tub.

Ma always kept the tub filled with water just in case the water was shut off in the morning or there was a fire like the one Benjamin and I started. As I ran through the French doors and down the hallway Ma spotted me running past her room with my hair in flames and jumped up to extinguish my burning hair. At the same time Pa's friends alerted him that flames were coming out of his living room window. They could see the flames from the side window a block away. Pa's friends came running to our apartment building from the social club.

Within seconds everyone in the apartment was up yelling, "Fire!" and passing pots of water. By the time the firemen arrived, the fire was out. While I sat in the hallway of the building with our neighbors, I patted my head and singed pieces of hair fell in front of my face into the palm of my other hand. I had no idea my hair had caught on fire. The side of my face was burned under the chin and Ma's left arm had a third degree burn. This was painful and embarrassing, but not the worst of it.

The worst part was Pa's attempt to discipline us. He beat Benjamin, Jerome and me with the broom that night like he beat Ma. If the three of us were running a race, the result definitely was a tie. Our punishment brought Benjamin and I closer together. My heart went out to Jerome, who had nothing to do with the fire but got the worst of the beating.

Jerome was actually in bed while the two rooms were going up in flames. Pa broke the wooden broomstick over his legs. Before the beating Pa argued with Ma, then took his anger out on the boys. It was Benjamin and I who caused the fire, not Ma. Both of us caused the embarrassment before the neighbors and Pa's friends. After the fire Pa's friends were very helpful.

It was especially good when Pa befriended the custodian at the local school who gave him boxes of leftover frozen dinners. He got boxes of a variety of dinners that Ma would pop in the oven on the days that she was too hung over to cook. We had salisbury steak and mashed potatoes with green peas, or hamburger with potato totters, for days. When Ma relied on the donated frozen dinners Uriel, Benjamin, Ruth, Flora, Melissa, Jerome, and myself combined our allowance and headed to the pizza shop for a slice or beef patty to share. Thank God we got an allowance.

I really do not now how Pa was able to give all eight children in the household a weekly allowance, but he did. This was the one thing I can say my father gave us when we were young. I really would have settled for an occasional hug or some kind of affection. Pa expected us to save our allowance to get whatever we needed. Whenever we needed additional money to finance something he always had the same question for us.

"What happened to the money I gave you?" he asked.

"I spent it," was our common response. He then went into his gambling money to give us additional money, knowing that he would get it back from Ma. He easily volunteered his money when we needed it for some special event or purchase, knowing Ma would eventually give it back to him, like the time Benjamin joined the Cub Scouts.

When Benjamin joined the Cub Scouts, everyone thought it was great. Pa even came up with the money to buy Benjamin a Cub Scout uniform. Benjamin attended all the meetings, sleepovers and marches. I also wanted to be part of something to get out of the apartment so I joined when the Cadets started a chapter at a local community center across from P.S. 144.

Uriel, Benjamin, Ruth, Flora, Melissa, Jerome, and I went there to get free lunch and play games. When the center placed a sign up sheet for the Cadets, I joined. I thought it was now my turn to shine like my brother did in the Cub Scouts. I really loved the uniforms the Cadets had. They were tan, not like the dark blue uniform Benjamin wore. Instead of the bright yellow scarf with the blue stripe around it and gold necktie the Cub Scouts had, the Cadets had a cool tan hat. The idea to join the Cadets to get away from Douglas' sexual abuse bothered me even more because I started becoming sexual with Benjamin.

Having sex with Benjamin was something that developed innocently. Most nights Benjamin and I talked before we went to bed. We just chatted about things that happened during the day or things that we wanted to do. This was something Benjamin did with his Cub Scout buddies when they had sleepovers.

One night we began talking about our bodies. The discussion intensified when we started discussing particular body parts then dared each other to measure and compare our penis size. Penis size is what seemed to make young boys think they were men. Another indication was if one had pubic hair. Benjamin was very proud of the faint hairs that were beginning to sprout on him.

"Mine is bigger than yours," he said.

"Oh yeah," I responded standing up to his challenge.

"Let me see yours," he said.

"Let me see yours," I said.

"Come here," I said.

"You come here," he said which gave me the signal to climb out of my bed to meet him in the middle of the room. We then took out our penises, playing with them first to make them hard. After making them hard, we did not have a ruler to measure them, so we leaned up against one another and pressed our penises together to compare their lengths. We each thought our penis was special and better than the other's because they each had a distinct look.

The first night we explored further. When our penises touched we were stimulated even more and played with each other. I was already experienced because of Douglas but this experience was different than the ones I had in the past. It was a secret form of innocent exploration desired by both parties involved. Benjamin and I continued to explore for a while.

Whenever there was a discussion at night before we went to bed, we ended up engaging in sexual play of some kind. I was glad Douglas stopped coming around at the time.

"If this is what the boys in the Cub Scouts did at night, I wanted to join, regardless of what the uniform looked like," I thought to myself after my first experience with Benjamin. With Benjamin, sexual play became fun and not scary like it was with Douglas in the late hours of the night or early mornings.

But it was too late, I had already filled out the permission slip to join the Cadets, and bothered Pa for the money to buy the Cadet uniform. Uriel and I went up the block to Pa's social club and interrupted a game of spades to ask him if he'd buy me a Cadet uniform. I was afraid to ask him because he did not like to be interrupted in the middle of a game of Spades, especially if he was losing. But I really wanted it so I asked.

"Pa, buy me a suit?"

"Huh?" he responded.

"Buy me a suit," I said.

"Soup?" he said.

"Yeah, a suit" I said.

The rest of the players gave me a stare as if they wished I would leave. My heart almost stopped when I saw my father tilt his body to the side and make the motion of reaching into his pocket. He pulled out a small wade of bills and started counting. Pa straightened them from their folded position. One, two, three, I waited patiently for I knew when he got closer to the middle of the fold there were five, tens, and twenties. All of a sudden the motion of his hands stopped at three. He pulled the three bills from the money and told me to go to the store and buy a box of soup.

"Get a box of Lipton soup," he said.

I took the money and walked out the club with my sister. Uriel and I went to Gill's grocery store on the corner and bought a box of Lipton soup. Going back to the club I gave the soup to my father and gave it another try.

"Pa buy me a suit?" He gave me back the bag with the box of soup in it.

"Here soup," he said.

I was crushed. Taking the bag from his hand, Uriel and I went home and when we got there went into the kitchen and I placed the soup on the kitchen table.

"What's in the bag?" Ma asked me when I placed the bag on the kitchen table and handed her the change.

"Michael asked Pa to buy him a suit and Pa sent him to by soup," Uriel told Ma.

When Pa got home that night the yelling started. Benjamin heard the door slam, pulled up his underwear, and quickly jumped back in his bed. We both were quiet pretending we were asleep.

"Why is that boy asking me for soup?" was the first thing my father said when he entered his bedroom.

"He was asking for a Cadet suit," Ma told him.

"What suit?" he asked. He still did not understand.

"A suit like you got Benjamin," she said.

"I have no money for a suit," he said as he left the bedroom and went into the kitchen and began banging pots to heat up some dinner. Lying in my bed, I thought of all the reasons why I did not get the money for my Cadet suit. I felt like crying but I did not, being as strong as Ma.

"Every time he asks you for something you never get it for him," Ma told him.

"For what?" he said.

"You don't even talk to him, what is wrong with you?" she asked.

Like always she was sticking up for me as she argued with my father when he returned from the kitchen. That night they argued but did not fight. Like she always said, if she had the money I knew she'd have gotten me that suit. After arguing with Pa, Ma started saving some of her money without Pa knowing.

That year she saved up so much money she was able to buy me combat boots for Christmas and made it a memorable holiday. Having the combat boots made me happy because I was prepared for the winter. It was December 1976 and New York had the blizzard of the decade. She also decided to get all of her children a musical instrument. Drum set, guitars, organ, bongos, maracas, tambourine, all of us were equipped so that together we formed a band. Ma must have been influenced by the life story of the Jackson Five, or else she got the idea from watching us and the neighborhood kids play our air instruments during the summer months in the empty lot next door.

The building next door was torn down and bulldozed to a flat piece of land. A group of neighborhood kids including myself set up a large piece of wook on empty milk crates that we got from Gill's store on the corner to make a stage. On our makeshift stage we also set up poles made from old broom sticks, like the one Pa beat Benjamin, Jerome and I with the night Benjamin and I set the fire, to use as microphones.

"I remember when rock was young. Me and Suzie had so much fun," I sang Elton John's hit as people passed by.

"Let me sing now," Andrew, my best friend who lived next door, asked as he tried to take the microphone away from me.

Andrew was a typical aggressive boy next door. He was very curious and always looking for a new adventure. He was light skinned with dark black hair and hazel eyes, standing about four feet five. Andrew and I explored our neighborhood when our parents gave us the freedom to roam. Our areas of exploration were beginning to increase with the increase in transients in our neighborhood.

The neighborhood was already a poor one, with people moving out quicker than they moved in leaving many abandoned apartment buildings that eventually forced the owners to abandon them, leaving hollow structures and room for ghosts in the neighborhood. Andrew and I were like Tom Sawyer exploring the Mississippi, but instead we explored abandoned apartment buildings, salvaging what past residents had left behind. Exploring the vacant depths of the South Bronx brought us closer together.

On two occasions we were chased out of an abandoned building occupied by the homeless. The fear and the energy of the chase left two sweaty boys standing side-by-side retelling the tale as we embraced on another. These events created a stronger bond between Andrew and I, and eventually led to the innocent type of sexual exploration that I experienced with Benjamin. Although we were close to one another at times we were at each other's throat.

"Let the song finish first, then you go next," I said while pulling the mike away from him.

"Give me a turn to sing," he said.

It was fun belting out those seventies tunes, the portable radio blaring out the music as we lip-synched the words. People stopped their cars to see our performance as they drove by. We did not think at the time to place a tip jar out to collect some extra change. Pa was usually the one to get a tip from his friends for his horse playing, but this time it was Ma. Looking out the kitchen window into the yard she saw how great our performances were and the possibility of becoming the next Osmond family. My family woke up a second after midnight. Ma's voice was heard throughout the apartment.

"Hannah, Uriel, Benjamin, Ruth, Flora, Melissa, Jerome, Michael, wake up Santa Claus came," she yelled, "Get up and see what Santa Claus brought you."

We all jumped up out of the bed and ran into the living room to the lopsided tree that was mutilated by my father. Ma did whatever she had to do to make sure we always had a good Christmas even though Pa cut down the Christmas tree each year with a machete and fought with her. My heart was filled with joy when I opened a triangular shaped present with a large gold bow on it that turned out to be a guitar. Beside me sat Benjamin with an identical shaped box but his had a red bow. One by one we opened our gifts to find a musical instrument, and we all began to play together. Hannah banged on her drums, Uriel played her bongos, Ruth played her electric organ, Flora blew into her flute, Melissa shook her maracas, Jerome hit his tambourine and Benjamin and I strummed on our guitars. What noise did we make!

That Christmas must have cost Ma a fortune because all the instruments were not toys– they were all real professional instruments. This was better than past Christmases. One Christmas, Ma did not have any money at all. It was a hard year as usual, but this time it was even harder. One of Ma's sisters, Aunt Rachel, who always brought gifts, was unable to come. I think Ma must have explained the situation to her oldest sister, Rochelle, since Aunt Rochelle took it upon herself to go to a thrift shop on Long Island and shop for toys to bring to us.

That Christmas I really felt poor. Aunt Rochelle walked into our apartment with two large black Hefty bags and her most sought after chocolate mint sheet cake. After settling in with a cup of coffee, she handed the bags to Hannah to distribute the unwrapped gifts to us. There were board games with missing pieces, baby dolls with matted hair, and parts of toys that were unrecognizable. I was losing hope, as Christmas seemed to be getting dull until we got our instruments.

The wood on my guitar glistened in the light. Its tight strings sent out notes as I stroked them with the colorful pic that came in the box with the instructions on how to take care of the guitar. But the care of the instrument and the happiness that went with it were very short lived.

Between Christmas and New Years, our instruments were destroyed in a fight between Ma and Pa. Three days after Christmas there was yelling and screaming about money. Pa was once again asking Ma for money. She did not have any; all she had was spent on our expensive gifts. He was upset that she did not have any money to give him, so he cursed the instruments then grabbed Benjamin's guitar to hit Ma. Ma grabbed mine to protect herself and in the brawl most of the instruments were destroyed.

The bases of the guitars were ripped off their handles, the drum skins were punctured and the rims were bent in, the skin of the tambourine was torn, the maracas were cracked, and the only two instruments that survived the fight were Ruth's electric organ and Uriel's pair of bongos. Even with the fight and loss of our gifts, no one can take away the few good moments of happiness that Ma brought us that Christmas.

When the Christmas holiday was over and I return to school we were required to write an essay about our holiday.

Instead of writing about the traumatic Christmas experience I wrote about how I received a new pair of boots. While talking to classmates I called attention to the new pair of combat boots I had and diverted the conversation to what it was like being in the Cadets. My feelings about being a Cadet that year and wanting to wear a uniform ended with the season but the feelings I was developing for sexual play and the abuse to continue did not.

When Douglas was not around to smother me with his body while I slept I had begun experimenting with Benjamin, and when Benjamin was not around my sexual feelings and desires turned to our dog Taxi. As little Taxi crawled onto my bed, I sucked on its nipples and play between its legs thinking that the stub between its legs would grow like Douglas and I did. The dog never grew because it was female. Not knowing what was happening to me, I was mimicking Douglas at night when the dog crawled onto my bed.

Benjamin and Jerome slept in the same room as me, so I expected that Douglas was also abusing Benjamin because of our sexual play. It did not occurr to me that Benjamin was learning from the same source as me to explain why he wanted to engage in sexual play at night. Benjamin gave me the impression that his form of sexual play was learned by spending time at sleepovers in the Cub Scouts. There was a major difference, however. Benjamin never attempted to act sexual with me while I was asleep. We were both conscious and aware of each other's behavior.

There was also communication between us prior to and during the sexual play that made the event mutual and innocent. We were both trying to learn from our experience, so I do not know if Douglas attacked Benjamin at night. When Douglas preyed at night he made sure everyone else was asleep, so Jerome and me may have been asleep in the den when Douglas preyed on Benjamin. It was not until later that I learned the truth.

It was not the sexual play that develops innocently between two children that was developing in my house. It was Douglas' unnatural kind of sexual play that was perpetuating among my family members. I was not Douglas' only victim. I did not know it at the time, but Douglas was preying on all of my brothers and sisters. He was moving from one family member to the next, from Hannah on down to Melissa.

Like a worker bee he moved from one flower to the next and his method was spreading like a weed. We were an innocent bunch being mowed down one by one, stripped of our innocence and in the process learning from it. Learning how to be sexually active on an autonomic level.

Chapter IV:
Man as Machine

The behavior that we began to exhibit towards each other as children seemed automatic. We were like programmed robots. One summer evening when everyone was supposed to be asleep, Uriel slowly opened the French doors of the den and crept into the room. Deep breathing was coming from Benjamin and Jerome's beds across the room—they were both asleep. Uriel came closer to my bed. It was Douglas who came to my bed at night, so I was surprised and didn't know what to expect.

"Michael, are you up," she asked.

"Yeah, why?" I said.

"Come with me," she said.

"Why?" I said.

She grabbed onto my arm and slowly tugged on it trying not to wake my brothers as she pulled me out of the bed. We quietly went down the hallway past my parent's room, kitchen, bathroom, and Hannah's room to the room Uriel shared with Ruth. Ruth was sound asleep on the top bunk bed. Uriel slowly got into her bed and pulled me in with her, covering us up with a wool blanket. She instructed me to lie on top of her, and then pulled my Fruit of the Looms down to my ankles. I felt heat radiating from the lower part of her body through her panties as our bodies rubbed against one another in the dark under the covers.

It was getting hotter and wetter the more we rubbed on each other. Uriel directed me all the way without words. This experience smelled sweaty and was very slippery. I began gasping for air; it was difficult to breathe under the wool covers. Every bed in the house had a knitted cover since crocheting was a pastime of my grandmother.

"Stop," I said afraid of falling off the bed.

Uriel was twelve years old and stronger. She held on to me and I trusted her. We did not consumate the experience that night because Ruth was on the top bunk bed and the creaking of the bed was beginning to wake her.

"Go back to your bed," she said.

I quietly returned to the other end of the apartment without being noticed. My penis was hard and protruding out of my underwear. When I passed my parents' room I covered the lower part of my body with my hand and turned sideways past their door. I thought to myself that if they asked what I was doing up I'd tell them I was using the bathroom. Not expecting such advances from Uriel, I was surprised at what happened and didn't really know what it was.

I had only experienced this with boys. Just like me Uriel had also learned a lesson that she began to practice at night. That night her panties were silky in a rough way. They were not the 100% silk but a polyester pair made from the fabric bought on sale at the clearance section in the basement of Alexander's the department store on Third Avenue in the Bronx.

When Ma's funds were low she went to the fabric store on Third Avenue and bought fabric to make clothes on the old Singer sewing machine she kept in her bedroom closet. I watched Ma as she cut out the pattern, using an old pair of panties, from her newly purchased fabric.

"Flora, come in here!" Ma yelled out.

"Yes Ma," Flora said as she entered my parent's bedroom.

"I need to measure the right amount of elastic to sew on to the edges of this fabric," she said to Flora.

Flora looked at my mother like she was keeping her from something important.

"My Flora you're not getting any taller," Ma said. "How old are you know?"

"I'm seven, Ma," she said with a tone of annoyance in her voice.

Although she was only seven, Flora was extremely petite and skinny, like a child suffering from malnutrition, even though she ate large portions of food at dinner. Her hair was fine and dark like the tone of her skin. Flora was very playful and spent much time joking around the house or arguing with me.

"Melissa, come in here right now!" Ma yelled.

"I'm coming!" Melissa yelled back from the living room.

Melissa entered my parent's bedroom huffing and puffing. Melissa was quite the opposite of Flora; she was very serious most of the time. She was six years old and physically much heavier than her older sister. Melissa too had a coffee-colored complexion though her hair was a much lighter ash brown. She had a distinguishing birthmark that ran down her chin that brought her much unwanted attention.

51

"This fabric looks good on you with your complexion," Ma said.

"Are you finished Ma?" Melissa asked.

"Not yet dear, I have to sew the elastic into the fabric," Ma said.

Not only was the material silky but it was very shinny and colorful. There was powdered blue, pink and a stripped pattern of black, white and golden yellow. I remember those specific colors because Flora and Melissa looked like little bumblebees buzzing around the apartment when they wore them. At the time Dubee was one of my favorite characters on the early morning television show *Romper Room*. I liked Dubee because everyone could understand the large bee without it saying a word. In the silence of my abuse, I often wished other people heard what I was thinking in my mind. In my magical thinking I wished that I could communicate what was happening to me.

It was similar to watching Ma place black disks into the old Singer sewing machine and watch it produce a new pattern. The simple changing of a disk helped give the machine a new instruction to create a new pattern in the fabric; a form of communication or information transfer without the use of words. It was the same as real pollinating bees that do not need spoken language because they do a little dance to communicate with other bees.

Flora and Melissa buzzed around the apartment in a dance, showing off their new panties, communicated to me how Ma was doing financially. On my mother's budget, Alexander's basement was the place to shop. We went shopping there with Ma weeks before school started. Three pants, five shirts, a pack of tube socks, a pair of sneakers, shoes, notebook, pencils, and bookbag seemed to last a lifetime.

By the time Fall came around Uriel visited my bed one more time, though instead of being led to her bedroom, the bathroom was the place of our next encounter. While everyone was sleeping she took me by the hand but this time led me to the bathroom. It was obvious to me that this was a strategy she learned from Douglas. Because the bed made too much noise, he must have took her to the bathroom. It was a move as cold and calculated as was the floor that night.

There in the bathroom two doors down from my parents' bedroom, I had intercourse on the bathroom floor with my sister. I had a dry orgasm but did not have the slightest idea what it was. My body trembled from the release of tension and the cold floor. When we were done she told me to go to my room. I was used to taking orders in a home that ran like a branch of the military. She was showing me a new form of sexual play and I easily followed her instructions.

Later on I took it upon myself to show this routine to Flora and Melissa but was unsuccessful. The two of them were seven and six. They were also dragged out of bed on different nights to the cold floor of the bathroom as I relived the experience I had with Uriel, but the event was not to be reenacted since their bodies were too young. At the age of eight I learned that I had a pretty developed body for my age.

Douglas's and Pa were also developed. In my eyes Douglas and Pa were men, something Pa never told or showed me how to be. Even with the experiences I had with my sisters and my best friend Andrew's twin sister as we played doctor, I never really had the desire to know a woman in the way I wanted to know a man. My initial experiences with men etched a space in my brain. This not only led me to experiment with Andrew's sister but with

53

Andrew himself, not getting very far since Ruth walked into the bathroom that afternoon and caught me trying to have sex with Andrew.

It was these experiences with boys that became part of the BIOS–the basic input/output–system of my mind. It was like a biochip had been formed in the gray matter of my brain instructing me to desire and respond sexually only to males. These experiences did not faze me. It was learning that Douglas was visiting my family once again that took a toll on my nerves. The savagery my brother inflicted upon us had stopped for a while and although he was away his abuse was still affecting the family.

Ma's alcoholism was also affecting the family. One night Ma drank so much that she became extremely depressed. She was feeling suicidal and threatening to kill herself. As children we really did not understand alcoholism and its effects. In our eyes, we saw our mother very sad, nodding over to the side and not being able to get up out of the kitchen chair. Being held up by the table as she rested her left arm against it and glancing at my grandmother's picture, her eyes filled with tears while my grandmother looked down on us from above.

"Ma is sick," Hannah told the younger children as we gathered in the kitchen.

"Ma is sick," we whispered back to one another.

When we were sick, Ma took care of us. While mending a wound or taking our temperature Ma comforted us with a soft tone.

"You're lucky I don't have to take you to the hospital," she'd say.

Ma's sickness was too much for us to handle, we did not know what to do for her so we decided to take her to the hospital. That night she was dressed in her blue jeans and a burgundy sweatshirt. I ran into her bedroom to get a pair of shoes to match her outfit. To complete the ensemble we had her put on her brown windbreaker then lifted her up from the chair to go to the hospital. As we lifted her up she grabbed for her beer that sat on the table. After an hour she was able to walk on her own without falling and agreed with us to go to Bronx Lebanon Hospital. Ma filled a shopping cart with items that we took with us.

With survival kit packed we headed to the hospital about midnight. All eight of us walked down the dark streets past Crotona Park. When we arrived, Ma was evaluated and received a prescription. The doctor looked at all of us.

"How many children do you have?" he asked Ma.

"Thirteen," Hannah quickly responded taking on the role of substitute parent.

He seemed amazed when Ma told him that we were all brothers and sisters. Ma always told the same story.

"I had twenty-two births and thirteen of my children survived," Ma said.

"God blessed you," the doctor replied looking in amazement.

I often asked myself, if it was a miracle, why was my life so miserable? Sometimes I wished someone would come and take me away to have a better life and that is just what Eva tried to do with all eight of us one summer.

That summer Eva came to the Bronx from Patchogue, Long Island, to visit. Eva was very tall and lanky. Her curly brown hair was as wild and uncontrollable as she was. Eva was on her own at a young age and had to learn from Mount Loretta how to be a lady, though the orphanages' attempts to control her were unsuccessful. It never failed. Ma usually received a phone call during the end of the week for her to come and get Eva for the weekend. Eva was a young woman now and still surviving on her own. She was doing well and it appeared that she wanted to help Ma.

During her visit Ma explained to Eva about her depression and drinking.

"Ma, what you need is a vacation," Eva said.

"Come on out to Long Island with me?" she asked.

Ma was delighted with the idea.

"I can't with all these kids," Ma said.

"Never mind the kids," Eva said, "We'll take them all with us."

My sister went on to explain to Ma how she just moved in to a huge new apartment with two large bedrooms, a large living room and a large back yard that we could all play in. Eva was very persistent and did not take no for an answer.

"OK, we'll all go, but only for a couple of days," Ma said.

"Great, Ma, you will get to relax," Eva said. Ma turned to Hannah.

"Hannah, tell everyone to pack their bags, we're going on vacation," Ma said.

We were told to pack enough clothes for a week. We all packed our bags that afternoon and headed out to Long Island.

When we arrived at Eva's apartment late in the evening we all went to bed so that we could get up early for breakfast the next morning. After breakfast Eva took us to Medford, Long Island, where Aunt Rochelle lived. Everything was fine until we got back to Eva's apartment that night. Eva and Ma began arguing about something in the kitchen. The argument escalated and resulted in the Patchogue police coming over and escorting Ma and Eva out of the house.

When Ma returned with Eva the next morning, Ma woke us up and told us that we were going back to the Bronx.

Later on Ma explained that Eva was trying to get her to transfer her welfare benefits over to Long Island so that Eva could get custody of all of us.

"Last night the police came to take Eva and I to a psychiatric hospital," Ma said.

"Eva tried to have you institutionalized?" asked Hannah.

"Yes," Ma replied.

Ma was evaluated at the hospital and in the process the evaluating psychologist contacted Ma's psychiatrist at Bronx Lebanon Hospital.

Ma's diagnosis of depression was the same. In addition, the doctor had concluded that she was not suicidal or dangerous to herself or the children. The doctor also concluded she was mentally competent to raise her own children and handle her own affairs. The doctor even questioned Eva's mental state. There was no need for Eva to try to shield us from Ma.

It was Ma's duty to protect us from evil in the world, even though she had failed to do so in her own apartment, but Eva did not know what was going on with Douglas. The abuse continued to flourish after we returned from Long Island and I believed it was my responsibility to protect Flora, Melissa and Jerome from Douglas, when I realized it was wrong.

* * * *

Even though I knew the sexual play was wrong and tried to protect Jerome from Douglas's abuse, I encouraged him to participate with me in my own escapades. My own behavior was encouraged by my notion of what we were supposed to do as boys that I learned from my male classmates. At

57

P. S. 144, all the boys in my third grade class talked about having sex with two sisters who attended the school. The two sisters had propositioned Jerome and I.

The older sister kissed and touched me while her younger sister worked on my little brother. Both sisters were known by most of the boys in school as a result of their promiscuity. There were rumors that they had sex with many of the boys. I met the older sister in the bathroom during reading lab one afternoon and was caught by the reading teacher but my parents were not notified.

The sisters met my brother and I one day after school and we fooled around in a parking lot across the street near the *Sharon Baptist Church*. This experience was exciting and frightening at the same time. We stopped seeing the sisters after this meeting, though I continued to seek out sexual experiences. My explorations also included Benjamin's friends who stayed over night in our apartment on the weekends.

It was puzzling not knowing if my brother's friends learned their behavior from Douglas or Benjamin, then decided to teach me, or if they learned this behavior in their own homes and were introducing it to me. It seemed to me most likely that Benjamin was also abused by Douglas and had introduced the behavior to his friends, and now it was coming full circle.

Regardless of its root, the newfound pastime was continuing to spawn like a weed. When Douglas came around this time to visit he tried it once again and realized that I was awake. Not only was I awake, but I became aroused as he pulled my underwear down, lifted my tee shirt and began humping on my lower back.

I learned that when he detected my penis was hard it stopped Douglas dead in his tracks. He would retreat at the awareness of victim arousal. It was like a computer detecting a virus. This was not part of his program, victims were not supposed to enjoy the experience. He had radar, detected arousal, and stopped functioning. After that night he stopped preying on me unless I remained an un-aroused docile body.

When he approached me the next time, I pretended I was asleep and stayed faced down lying on my stomach so the erection did not give me away. Snoring louder when he approached at night was a signal I gave off indicating to him that I was asleep and this led him to come straight to me and pull off my underwear. It was like I was learning how his system worked and how to control it; accessing his central processing unit was a breeze. Knowing that he had gotten to my older sisters and then to me, it was obvious to me that the next ones in line were Jerome, Flora and Melissa. But how did I know? Learning his methods, I attempted to prey on them when he was not around.

Abusing the older children was no longer stimulating for Douglas. Seeing that his victims were aroused turned him off. He repelled from those aroused like two positive poles of a magnet. Douglas was now drawn to neutral, innocent objects. Realizing early that what I attempted to do was wrong and Flora, Melissa and Jerome were next in the flow of events, I wanted to protect them. The predator was going for my baby sisters and brother next so I had to stop him. Instinctively knowing that Flora was next I wondered how I could help her. My true motivation was to keep the abuse to myself. It was jealousy that motivated me, I wanted the sexual play only for myself so I came up with a plan.

During the day I spent more time with my sisters to learn from them. I learned from the oldest to the youngest what it was to be a girl. A large part of being a girl appeared to be dressing up, applying makeup and smelling nice. I realized if I played dress up I gained lots of attention.

One evening Uriel, Benjamin, Andrew and I were all in Uriel and Ruth's room sitting on the lower bunk bed talking about our plans for the summer when the door to the apartment opened and Douglas walked in. When I saw it was he, I quickly took an old silky green and black curtain that once adorned the windows and draped it around me like the Statue of Liberty. I then begged Uriel to put my hair in her hot rollers and make up my face. Uriel started banging on her bongos as I danced around the room hoping to get Douglas's attention. We were not loud enough so I put on the radio to play some music and then I danced around while everyone in the room cheered. The noise brought Douglas back to us.

I thought the image of a feminine beauty would get Douglas's attention. It worked. When he saw me he stormed into the room and tried to grab at me. I quickly hit the floor and rolled under the lower bunk bed.

"Leave him alone," Uriel said.

"He's not bothering you," Benjamin said to Douglas.

"What's his problem?" said Andrew.

"Ma, Douglas is bothering Michael!" Uriel yelled.

Being coquettish and coy were qualities I learned from my sisters to attract the attention of an out of control male who was on sexual overdrive. When he saw me I wanted him to want me, not Flora, Melissa or Jerome. Douglas grabbed me and tried to pull me from the bed but could not. I held on to the wooden slab that prevents the mattress from falling through the frame. Douglas let go of me and left the room.

It took a while before he returned, and meanwhile I took off the makeshift dress and wiped the makeup off my face.

Douglas's drive was so fixed on his desires that he did not think of the feelings of others, just his own. He was enraged when he left the room, and I was afraid of what he would do to me if he got to me.

My behavior seemed to get to him. He was in such a state that it appeared he was malfunctioning. The idea of seeing me as a woman did something to him. He did not like it. Was I ugly as a woman? That was possible, but everyone else in the room seemed to like how I looked. Could it be that I represented an object that could not be penetrated? While I was young he never did penetrate me, so what could it have been? Was I too late? Had he already tried to penetrate Flora and Melissa and learned like I did earlier that that wasn't possible?

No, I had penetrated his system and he realized that I knew what he wanted. He wanted my little sisters and brother for his next victims but he saw the decoy in me and sensed something. He sensed that I knew his next move. My behavior was becoming as automatic as his, though I was one step ahead of him. I processed the events and predicted successfully what his next move was going to be. Acting like a pawn in the game of chess, I was able to place my evening playmate in check.

Chapter V:
Refining Automaton

E very morning we awoke to my mother's voice like waking to an alarm clock.

"Time to get up," she yelled.

We all arose automatically and headed for the bathroom to wash up. Full baths were taken in the evening so that the bathroom was not congested in the morning.

"Do not forget to brush your tongue," she called as she laid out our clothes for the day on our beds and then returned to the kitchen to prepare our breakfast.

Breakfast was sometimes served in front of the television but this practice was discontinued as I got older. I learned my A, B, C's and 1, 2, 3's from *Sesame Street*. The basics were mastered in front of the television, but it was for society's institutions to teach the rest. To me, it seemed like the educational system kept score in the form of report cards to help distinguish what Plato's *Republic* called the bronze, silver and gold souls or to separate the wheat from the chafe as the *Bible* states. In retrospect it appeared that the educational system was a cleansing as well as a training process.

After washing up it was then time to put on our uniforms. All three boys had the same outfits. The only time there was a difference in outfits was when the same color of a shirt or pant was not available in our sizes. Looking like a clone was not fun. Dressing children like this was usually saved for identical twins. We looked like triplets from the neck down.

When one of us grew out of his outfit it was still large enough for the next smallest boy to wear it. I felt sorry for Jerome, who wore the same outfit for years. Not only did he get my old clothes, he got to wear the outfits Benjamin outgrew as they were handed down through me. The practice of hand me downs seemed to reinforce a certain way of being. It prolonged traditions, making daily life appear like deja vu to me and I am absolutely sure to others when I arrived at school.

In 1979 when I was in the sixth grade my attendance and grades were excellent. This was not the case for Hannah, Uriel, Benjamin, and Ruth. Douglas's sexual abusive behavior was taking a toll on them. My attempt to get Douglas to prey on me only was not affective. My brothers and sisters were unable to keep their head above water; I helped Flora, Melissa, and Jerome jump ship by having them stay in after school programs to protect them. They were persuaded to join the track team to keep them busy and out of the house.

Participating in these events protected us from any abuse that occurred if we got home early. Anything was better than being at home. School became a refuge but unfortunately school did not protect us totally from the abuse at home. During this time I was about to graduate from P.S. 144 and life improved for the whole family. Luckily for all of us Douglas moved to Colorado that year.

After Douglas was gone, Ma's case manager told her about a new apartment building called Bronxville Houses just built on 156th Street and St. Ann's Avenue. My mother was still drinking at the time and her relationship with my father had not improved. It took the move to a new building for us to begin to live a more civilized existence.

Bronxville Houses was identical to the shelter that Robert Desjarlais describes in his book *Shelter Blues*. It was a new form of architecture designed to shape the lives of its participants and weed out any undesirable behavior. The apartment was a dream come true. It had ten rooms: five bedrooms, two bathrooms, a kitchen, a separate dining room, and a living room. The rooms still had to be shared but I did not care. Everything was new and beautiful.

The building was also safe. There was a security camera, and a security guard that patrolled the building. The intercom system allowed us to see a visitor as they entered the building. Bronxville also had maintenance men who kept the building and grounds clean. It appeared to me that all mechanisms were in place to give off the image that certain ways of living were not allowed. The building was built for a class of people who are more refined. The plush lawns of the new building at the Bronxville Houses were finely manicured. The building represented a new start for my family.

A new school, a new place to live and with Douglas out of the picture, it felt like life was about to begin. Little by little we filled shopping-carts with our personal belongings and pushed them three blocks and down the hill to our new place. Ma and Pa were arguing about the move.

"Were leaving," she said to Pa.

"Yeah, get out of my face," he said not believing her. The move was very spur of the moment and we did not believe her ourselves but we did what she told us.

"When I say were going, were going," she said and boy did we go.

There really was not much that we could carry in the carts besides small items and things made of fabric, like clothing. We moved in the evening. After my father realized that my mother was serious he started taking apart the bunk beds and dresser draws from the dresser and started filling up the station wagon. Pa did not spend the first night with us in the new apartment but joined us when the other apartment only had left the things that were not wanted. Ma seemed to want her beer for there was a case of it in the refrigerator of the new apartment. She drank as we all moved things in.

The first night we stayed in the new apartment, when the last shipment of items made its way over Flora, Melissa, Jerome and I began unpacking. We were told to stay with Ma in the new apartment while Hannah, Uriel, Benjamin, and Ruth continued to pack and move the furniture. As we unpacked boxes of sheets and curtains to put in the linen closet my mother stumbled into the back room where all four of us were. As usual she had had too much to drink.

"You kids make me sick. I'm going to kill you," she said this as she held a curtain twisting it around her hands in a slow motion.

As she approached I blocked Flora, Melissa, and Jerome.

"No Ma, please!" they shouted.

She got closer then she stopped and turned around and went into the kitchen to get another beer. After a while we dared to creep into the living room and as we peered in the dining room there she was, sleeping in a chair. We returned to the back bedroom together. We were too young to die. After that experience with Ma we had a hard time falling asleep. The next morning Ma acted like nothing happened, it was business as usual. We had to get to school that day.

In time life was getting better. I graduated from P.S. 144 to Intermediate School 161. Douglas was hundreds of miles away from the family in Colorado and didn't visit. He was gone and so was my mother's drinking and smoking habit. Miraculously Ma gave up drinking and smoking during the first few months in our new apartment. It definitely had a lot to do with her becoming a born again Christian.

"I gave it all up to the Lord," she said. "The Lord took it from me, I saw the burning bush that Moses saw."

Ma claims she saw sparks and flames shooting out of her chest and from that day on she lost the desire to drink and smoke. Her stories were very influential and the lessons I was being taught in I.S. 161 also had an impact on my life. At I.S. 161 the students were taught about a kind of energy that was going to revolutionize the world. Robotics was going to take man farther than the machines of the industrial revolution. We also learned about nuclear energy, fossil fuels and the refining process. Being in I.S. 161 was very confusing for me. I wanted to learn, but there was something else causing confusion. Getting through the seventh grade was difficult for me.

Getting close to a few of my classmates helped. One in particular made me feel very special inside. I became infatuated with him and just wanted to be with him, cherishing the times we sat next to each other in math class. Getting to know him made getting an education fun. He made the seventh grade worthwhile.

The eighth grade was just the opposite. The friends that I had made the previous year were no longer in my homeroom. My classmates and I were separated as a result of our academic abilities. But we did get the opportunity to see each other in certain classes. The infatuation that I developed for the boy who sat next to me in math class did not go away. Douglas was not around either, and it was quite a relief, but I missed the sexual play and began to be confused about my sexuality. Having strong sexual feelings for the boy in school conflicted with the Christian lessons Ma began to teach me.

Every morning after going through the routine of getting ready for school, I left the apartment in a rush to give the impression that I was going to school. Instead of going to school, I walked up the stairs and stayed on the top landing above the ninth floor that led to the roof until three o'clock. When it was three, I headed down to the apartment and knocked on the door as if I had just returned from a long school day. After a while, hiding in the staircase was no longer an option if I did not want to get caught.

While hiding I occasionally was seen by the maintenance man who cleaned the building each morning. Every time he saw me I was sure he told Pa. Pa became friends with him a few days after we moved into Bronxville. One block east of St. Ann's Avenue was P.S. 177 which had a park behind it. I decided after being seen too many times by the maintenance man that this park was a better place to hide.

One morning I sat on the same park bench as I always sat shivering in the cold. As I sat shivering, a young guy approached me.

"How are you doing?" he asked.

"Fine, just a bit cold," I said.

"You look familiar. Wait a minute, I know your sister," he said with a look of surprise on his face.

"You have a sister that goes to Jane Adams, right?" he asked.

"Yes," I replied.

Uriel was a student at Jane Adams High School at the time. At first, I was nervous when he approached me, but after he said he knew Uriel I felt more comfortable with him.

"You look cold in that purple jacket," he said, "Do you want to go for a walk?"

"OK," I said.

"Walking around will keep you warm," he said.

"Alright," I said feeling more trustful as we headed north in the direction of Jane Adams High School.

P.S. 177 and the park were built on a hill so when we reached the top of the hill we turned onto Jackson Avenue and went east until we were on Trinity Avenue. We walked to my old neighborhood, stopping in front of Gill's store that was a few doors down from the social club Pa frequented and right across the street from an abandoned P.S. 21. My old building at 158th Street and Jackson Avenue could be seen at an angle and was almost abandoned. As my new friend and I headed north on Trinity Avenue I began to feel a bit uneasy. Something just did not seem right.

When we reached half way down the block we came to a halt and were standing in the front of the entrance to P.S. 21.

"You want to go inside to look around?" he asked.

"Yeah, OK," I said.

Curious to see what the school looked like on the inside, I followed him in. As I entered the school after all those years, something caught my attention. The gargoyles were staring down on me. Remembering the morning of my first day of school, I raised my head to stair back at their faces, though this time it was different. The expressions on the gargoyles faces were hollow. They looked as empty as the school building. Soon after the school closed in 1975, the building was vandalized; much of its contents were stolen and the building itself was physically destroyed.

I followed my new friend through the debris as we entered the large metal doors. He directed me to an empty classroom on the second floor, room 201, the same class room that I was in with Ms. Green the first day Ma brought me to school. I did not let him know this. When inside room 201 my new friend approached me face to face and began pressing himself up against me as I stood their stiff as a board.

"Have you ever done this before?" he asked.

"No," I said.

The fact that I led him to believe the situation was new to me excited him even more. He opened his coat and his pants were bulging before him below his navel. Little did he know I was not new to this sort of experience. I knew this game and sensed that it was coming the moment he asked me to enter the abandoned school building with him. When I was younger living on Jackson Avenue, Andrew and I searched through abandoned buildings, but went in with the intentions of looking for old furniture or stuff that people left behind that was still in good condition and could be used.

Andrew never asked me to enter an abandoned building the way this guy did. I already knew by his tone what was in the Pandora's box before me. As he opened the buttons of my jacket, then the buckle of my pants, I just stood there and let him use me, giving me the same sensation that comes over me when I remember my earliest memory. He then quickly zipped up his pants and closed his jacket as I slowly composed myself. Turning away from me he headed towards the classroom door and left the building. All I thought to do was follow.

"See you later," he said when we left the school building.

As he walked away he turned to me and waived his hand walking in the direction of Jane Adams High School. My hand reflex kicked in and I raised my hand in a goodbye gesture. The school day was not over so I went back to the park bench behind P.S. 177 feeling not only cold, but also used and disgusted. I stayed there until it was time to return home. When I got home I quickly washed my hands and changed my soiled clothing.

The dirty event that took place that day just added to my confusion and took away from the pleasure of learning that I received in school buildings. I seemed to be getting myself in dangerous situations and not taking control of my actions. I didn't like getting myself into abusive situations, and I didn't like the state that I was in. Letting strangers take advantage of me, Douglas's abuse, being attracted to my male classmate, this was all coming to a head and the only way to get out of the turmoil was to weed myself out of life.

* * * *

My anger was suppressed for so long that it turned into depression. When I got home I went into the second bathroom that Pa used and took out a Gillette razor, wrapped it in toilet paper and hid it in my jacket pocket. With no place to go and not having anyone to talk to about my situation, I sat on a park bench in back of Bronxville Houses.

Hardly anyone was out that afternoon. It was a cold winter day. I saw a couple that lived directly below my family on the fifth floor entering the building. As I looked down on the ground I took a deep breath and a cloud of white smoke exited my mouth from the cold air. This prompted me to look up to the sky at the clouds and ask "Why?" I was desperate for an answer and a solution.

Reaching in my jacket pocket I feel the wrapped razor. I took out the razor, unwrapped it, raised my jacket sleeve and began to cut my left wrist. A small drop of blood apprared as I slowly pressed the razor into my forearm above the nerve. My focus on the spot was so strong that I did not feel any pain from the incision. At that moment I thought I had already made the decision to die, but then I heard the chirping of a group of sparrows in a tree behind me.

"Stop!" I heard the sparrows crying out to me. Then *His Eye is on the Sparrow*, a song Ma use to sing which tells of God's eye being on a sparrow and watching over his children came to me.

"We all are God's children," I heard Ma's voice tell me.

I stopped pressing the razor into my arm and took the tissue I had wrapped the razor in and pressed it against the cut. I realized those birds were trying to tell me something. They wanted me to know that I was part of a greater plan. I began realizing what society wanted me to be and what was the design to follow.

"God made man in his image," I heard Ma's voice again ring in my ear.

This was something she constantly told us as part of her newfound Christian teachings. In this view, it was man's plan for man to be like God in every way. In my case correcting myself and becoming civilized involved no longer engaging in any type of sexual play. Ma taught that the soul was cleansed by asking for forgiveness of one's sins. The only one I thought truly needed correcting and cleansing was Douglas, because of what he taught me at such a young age.

Douglas had a certain power over me. If he was in my presence or if his name was mentioned, it had an effect on me; I felt my whole being was in danger. My body froze whenever his name was mentioned. I felt as if all one had to do was say his name and I physiologically reacted. This made sense to me since Douglas means "dark". In understanding Ma's teachings I rationalized that he must have been a fallen angel.

The stories of angels are written into the *Bible* in layers. The first mention of angels in the *Bible* is when a cherub is placed in front of the tree of life after Adam and Eve eat from the tree of knowledge of good and evil. The apocalyptic apocryphal *Book of Enoch* tells us of the fallen angels who came to earth and engaged in sexual acts resulting in their lot of no peace. It was the fallen angels who were believed to perpetuate sin and evil on earth. Knowledge of God's design, angels, and the human soul helped me to cleanse my own soul and from that time on try to live an honest, true and refined life.

Chapter VI:
The Fallacy of Man

That I was not living the truth became clear when I listened closely to my inner self. My inside did not reflect who I appeared to be on the outside. I was living a falsehood. No longer wanting to hide the truth, I decided by the time I was in junior high school that I was going to reveal it. The only one I was deceiving was myself if I continued to have sex with Benjamin and hide what I knew about Douglas. But who was I and what was I becoming? To know the truth and straighten out my life I had to know who and what Douglas was.

I thought I could live a "straight" life like Benjamin, and be what I thought I wanted to be. Learning from Douglas that sexuality was a tool of control, I felt that it was better to use it for the good and not hide it. Sexuality is not only for secret pleasure. I came to believe that the knowledge of the power of sexuality and the pleasure of knowing knowledge que knowledge, in the manner of how Michel Foucault described the power/knowledge relation in his book *Power/Knowledge*, was the key to life.

Unfortunately, this knowledge did not explain the reason why I was born, why my life was the way it was, and most importantly, why I was being abused. I did not want to be like Douglas, but I grew fond of the sexual play so I worked on myself by focusing on the pleasure that I got from learning and attempted to become someone new.

Taking an interest in science I focused on memorizing the periodic table and the properties of the elements. We now knew more than the ancient Greeks; the philosopher Thales only fathomed water being the creative substance of the universe. The early philosopher Plato looked inside while Aristotle looked outside the body, and continued debating over the nature of the creative force that made the universe. Of what did it consist? There were atoms, protons, electrons, mesons, and quarks for those who study it today on the exterior and, neurons, genes or DNA for those studying the inside. I felt a body of knowledge was stored in me. This was not just the discovery of my mind but also the realization of a power that transcended the physical.

When I was a child, I believed I had the power to read minds. I knew little of the mind's power and its workings. Having this false belief did not help because I was unable to read Douglas' mind and was unable to tell when he was coming for a visit.

"You know your brother is coming from Colorado this weekend," Ma told me as I sat in the dining room.

"He is?" I asked.

"Yes, for Eva's house warming/family reunion," she said.

Sure enough he was back from Colorado to visit and the abuse continued. It started up again that rainy afternoon weekend. Eva bought a new house and invited everyone out for the house warming/family reunion. Everyone hopped in

Pa's station wagon and headed out to Long Island early that day.

We arrived at the house by noon, parked the car and headed toward the house to the large backyard, where Ma's sisters Aunt Rochelle, Rachelle and Roxana sat in plastic hunter green lawn chairs drinking iced tea in the faint sun that tried to peek through the clouds. Douglas was there and he saw me climb out the back seat of the car and cross the yard. My niece Theresa was chasing my cousin Colin across the lawn. As he talked to my relatives, he turned his head and saw that I was there. Oh so quickly did he make his way through the crowd to approach me. My heart began to beat quicker and I felt like hunted prey.

He stood before me with a insincere grin on his face. I was much older than he remembered and also now much wiser. I.S. 161 had opened up a whole new world to me and I now had a body of knowledge with wich he couldn't compete, since he left school at an early age. I wondered if he was up to old tricks. Less than ten minutes into the visit, I realized the game he was using to prey on my younger relatives.

"Want some soda?" he asked me.

The only thirst I had was the thirst to figure out what made him tick. I needed to figure out the answer to this question. The answer to the question was in the chaotic life that was before me. What new game had he devised, I asked myself having a hunch what he was up to.

"Yeah," I said.

"Soda," was the name of the new game he devised, I thought to myself. All the drinks for the children were in a refrigerator in the garage.

"Come I'll show you," he said and led the way.

I followed him around the side of the house to the garage entrance. Through the door and past some boxes stood a white refrigerator. He stepped ahead of me and kindly opened the door. The bottom of the refrigerator was filled with two cases of soda.

"I want a ginger ale," I said.

"There deep in the back," he said.

When I drank ginger ale, it made me feel like a grown-up. Children drank cola, and thinking I was an adult, I had to have something to differentiate me from the children believing that just the act of holding an adult drink made one resemble an adult. As I reached down to get a soda, Douglas stepped behind me and I began feeling him in an aroused state upon my backside. Quickly grabbing a *Coca-Cola*, I stood up and headed out the garage door. He still had control over me; I was still a child playing his games. He quickly followed pulling his shirt over the front of his pants to cover up his erection.

Although his face appeared calm and lacked emotion, his body was excited. His gonads were secreting testosterone putting him in a state of arousal. My mind was also aroused, but with curiosity. This experience was different than the earlier ones. Douglas was not afraid of getting caught. His emotion was like the nervousness of a child trying to get its way and not expressing that there was anything wrong with his desires.

He was more like Levi than I originally believed. This time Douglas' behavior was similar to Levi's when Levi played with me when Ms. Green took the class to the bathroom. This experience was getting me closer, but closer to what?

I headed for a large willlow tree far off in a remote area of Eva's yard. I found a spot and sat under the huge weeping willow yards away from my family, my thoughts beginning to race. My heart pounded as I tried to discern the truth. Douglas was a fallen angel, I thought to myself, as tears streamed down my face.

Douglas was evil, there was no question about it, but he was evil in a way that seemed innocent, as if he was an error of nature – not the result of learned experience like I originally expected – resulting from his experiences at St. Joseph's orphanage.

Besides there was no proof that he himself was the victim of abuse at St. Joseph's. Regardless of the question of evil and how to detect it, sexual abuse is a crime. Douglas had to know then that what he was doing now at his age was against the law. Maybe he could be forgiven for what he did when he was young, but he was an adult now. Sitting there under the tree I thought most adult victims of sexual abuse must suffer from Post Traumatic Stress Disorder (PTSD) and remain a child mentally. Their mental development remains stagnant, specifically in the area of conscience development.

The soul, or core value system of sexually abused children does not fully comprehend right from wrong in sexual matters. The idea of sex may be simultaneously associated with fear and pleasure. From my experiences with Douglas I grew to believe that the traumatic event of sexual abuse changes a person and the way they think. Although there was no proof, I was sure this is exactly what happened to Douglas as a result of his being abused in St. Joseph's. It is possible that he was just mimicking the suffocating behavior he learned in St. Joseph's.

"Hey Michael, what are you doing all the way over here," asked Uriel as she approached the huge willow pushing the branches out of her way coming towards me.

"Thinking," I said as I wiped my face.

"Are you crying?" she asked as she sat beside me.

"Yeah, I want to get away from here," I said.

"I know I hate these family things too," she said.

"Everyone is so phony and pretending they are so happy, I'm sick of it," I said.

"I'm sick of it too, Michael, but we just got here," she said.

"No body talks about how they really feel," I said.

"I know," she said and sat with me in silence.

I wanted to ask her about the night she took me to her bed, the night on the bathroom floor, and what Douglas just did to me, but I was too ashamed. She'd understand where I was truly coming from and why I sat crying under the willow tree. Uriel and I had experienced the loss of consciousness as a child while in the process of being molested by Douglas.

As we both lay in bed while we were children, Douglas used us both as our faces were smothered in the pillow. He did this continuously prior to the age of five and as we got older. Our bodies were being conditioned to lose consciousness and dissociate. This process was classically conditioned to sexual behavior and the pleasure that goes with it as we grew older, and the loss of consciousness in the process of the abuse was a result of a loss of energy to our brain due to circulatory insufficiency of our cerebral blood flow, a process that prevents the development of neurons required for conscience.

Uriel would also understand that Douglas had a mind programmed without a conscience. He was confused and not accepting what is morally right and wrong and instead gave himself over to satisfy bio-force urges. Later on in life I learned that when a victim of sexual abuse recalls the events, cerebral blood flow decreases, creating less energy and causing a loss of consciousness.

This phenomena has been demonstrated in samples of sexual abuse victims so presumably would hold for the sexual predator who also has been abused. The result of cerebral blood flow loss to the region of the prefrontal cortex prevents the development of morality neurons and the predator becomes what Robert Hare later described in his book with the same title as *Without Conscience.*

The longer I studied Douglas the more I found a way to his damaged core or soul. As I got older and continued reading to find out more about what I was dealing with, I came across Fred Alan Wolf's *The Spiritual Universe: How Quantum Physics Proves the Existence of the Soul,* an attempt to prove the existence of the soul. Unfortunately Dr. Wolf retracted his idea of writing a "proof book" after it was already published, his reason being that "the scientific community was not ready for his ideas as a proof of the soul's existence".

This reminded me of Claude-Adrien Helvetius' *De l'Esprit*, a philosophical but sensationalist discourse that attracted immediate attention and was condemned by priests who believed it was full of the most dangerous doctrines. The author, terrified at the time and fearful of the controversy he created, wrote three separate retractions. The book was publicly burned by order of the French Parliament in 1759.

Helvetius had three main principles. First, that all man's powers were reducible to physical sensation, even memory, comparison, and judgment. Second, that self-interest, established on the love of pleasure and the fear of pain, is the sole spring of judgment. Third, that all minds are equal and that their clear inequalities are due to the unequal desire for instruction, and this desire springs from the passions, of which all men commonly well-organized are vulnerable to the same degree. The key point of his thought was that public ethics has a functional basis.

It was Helvetius' main work and the only one to be published in his lifetime. This was one of two of his books that evoked an outcry from the religious and civil authorities and gained such universal public interest. The book was damned as atheistic, materialistic, sacrilegious, immoral and subversive. Helvetius' *De l'Esprit* lost its right to be published because its pages possessed all of the scandals scattered through the literature of its time.

Borrowing from Plato's *Republic*, Wolf's *The Spiritual Universe* explains the evils of the soul. A soul's specific evils include primary moral wickedness, intolerance, injustice, ignorance, guilt and is equivalent to psychological illness. Evil's primary goal is to render an object's order into chaos. It is an anti-God since it goes against good orderly direction (GOD).

The soul is not capable of being destroyed though it can be damaged. Like a damaged computer disk that does not allow a file to be saved, the sexual predator can commit acts of violence and not feel any guilt, because the same development of language used to manipulate symbols, transmit thoughts and information to others, and the notion of evil is not ingrained in the socialization process to indoctrinate guilt, sin, culpability, ego, etc. as a result of the abuse.

Getting a sexual predator to have a conscience is the same as trying to open up a computer file in the wrong program. The file cannot open because the software does not understand the symbolic language of the file. In the mind of a sexual predator the neural connections are not there to transmit the signals that hold the moral codes of conscience.

The solution is to develop an anti-virus program to help rid the sexual predator of his predatory behavior. Hopefully a program can be developed and combined with psychopharmacology to stimulate cerebral blood flow and soften the conscious awareness system of the sexual predator, so that moral codes can be etched in the gray matter of the brain. This is less intrusive than implanting a brain stimulation unit. Programming the sexual predator with moral training will help heal the damaged soul. I believe this treatment solution will be feasible in the not too distant future.

"It's time to go," Uriel said.

"Thank God, time flies when you're having fun," I said as Uriel and I stood up from under the willow tree.

"I'm hungry, are you?" I asked.

"Yeah, we didn't eat anything all day," she said.

"I'm sure Ma took some food home," I said.

"Yeah we can eat on the way home," she said.

Uriel and I quickly made rounds to say good-bye to everybody and headed for the car.

"Uriel, hold a seat for me in the back of the station wagon near the cooler," I said.

"Where are you going?" she asked. "Pa started up the car."

"To the bathroom to pee, I drank a cola when we got here," I said.

"Hurry up," she said.

Quickly running into Eva's house I shot up to the second floor bathroom then ran out to the car and hopped into the back. Pa pulled out of the driveway as we all waved good-bye.

"Give me a call when you get home," Eva shouted to Ma as we drove away.

"Bye," everyone in the car shouted as I sat in the back seat looking for something to eat.

A clear Tupperware container held different types of sandwiches. I popped open the lid, reached in and pulled out a ham and cheese.

"Uriel, you want a sandwich?" I asked.

"Yeah, what kind are there?" she replied, looking squeezed up against the cooler in the back of the car.

"Here's a turkey and cheese," I said as I handed it to her.

"Want something to drink?" she asked.

"Yeah," I said, "Is there any ginger ale?"

"No, only Coca-Cola," she said.

Hesitating for a moment, I looked out the window as our car passed by others on the Long Island Expressway, shifting my eyes up to the partly cloudy sky – it looked as if the storm clouds were following us.

"Michael!...Michael!"

"Yeah," I said.

"Do you want soda or not?" she asked.

"Yeah, cola," I said as I returned to looking at the storm clouds following the station wagon. I quietly thought to myself whether or not one believes it, I was sexually abused once again-the product of a corrupt soul?

Chapter VII:
The Golden Soul

I began to refine my soul. The events of my past had damaged it but they did not crush my spirit. Once again I made it to graduation. I attended the ceremony but when I got the official report card it was stamped transfer to Alfred E. Smith High School and not accompanied by a diploma. Since my attendance from the last year in Junior High School was poor, I was not good enough to merit the title of graduate since I missed most of the program. It was a reflection of the inner being of someone living without the software needed to be a success in life.

Alfred E. Smith High School was on the same block as Bronxville Houses. The entrance to the school is ten feet away from the apartment building. The architecture of the building is very plain and flat. There are no gargoyles at the top of the building to protect it like P.S. 21.

The bleak architecture of the building told that there was nothing special about the place and that the quality of the education offered was poor. At the time I wanted a state of the art education. I found what I wanted one day while reading a *Daily News* article by Dave Mendel titled, "Chancellors-Back-to-School Specials." The article explained that District 2 in East Harlem was starting a new pet program of the District Chancellor. He believed a miracle in East Harlem was possible and his fight for choice in public education was vindicated when the success of his pet project was documented in a 1993 book *Miracle in Public Education*.

At that time I felt like I really needed a miracle. Attending Alfred E. Smith H.S. was not going to provide me with the latest program being taught in the high schools for advanced students. My tarnished soul needed to be polished and my software needed to be updated. My physical being was atoms, protons, neutrons, electrons, mesons, and quarks, so I wanted to become a engineer when I was in Junior High School. I had taken the high school exam for the Bronx High School of Science but was told that I missed the cut off by one point.

Alfred E. Smith H.S. did not have the resources to provide a rigorous scientific education that would make me a high functioning data gatherer. At the time I began to believe that our government put into place systems, such as the educational system, to train individuals to become data gatherers by acting as compilers to feed the system with experiments to improve its body of knowledge. This methodology made use of knowledge and the power that comes with it in hopes to refine a previous body of knowledge to possibly crack the cosmic code and understand what Paul Davies described as *The Mind of God* in his book of the same title.

The *Bible* teaches us that when man and woman ate from the tree of the knowledge of good and evil that they have "all knowledge," a level man has not achieved since all we do know is, as Ma says, that God works in mysterious ways.

One biblical footnote of the version I read stated having all knowledge entailed "putting two opposites together like Genesis I:I, heaven and earth". I strongly believe the act of putting the building blocks of a language together or deconstructing them can lead man to have all knowledge and can be found in the breath of life or the spoken word. The Greeks called this the logos. I learned the building blocks of this sacred language when I was placed across the street in Public School 21. It is this language that has guided my life's journey.

So I took the article from the *Daily News* and called The Manhattan School for Science and Mathematics (MSSM), the Chancellor's pet project in East Harlem. The guidance counselor who took the call set up an appointment for the following week. Ma and I were running all over New York City looking for a new school for me to attend. MSSM was the final school we visited, and it was worth the wait.

My first semester's report card from Alfred E. Smith H.S. was transferred. The grades were poor but I passed and was admitted to the school. This was a moment to be proud. I had the desire to improve my situation and I took the chance. This was not sheer luck. Acting on the world, I was learning that I got results. My actions did not put me in situations, my actions helped create them.

It was up to me to create the life that I wanted and I was sure that I did not want Douglas in my life. In 1983 while I was in the 10th grade, Douglas returned to New York from Colorado. He did not know that our family moved and went looking for us at the old place on Jackson Avenue. By then the building was 99% empty. He asked the remaining occupants if they knew where we had moved.

Andrew's mother gave Douglas directions and one day he arrived at our new apartment before I got home from school. When I walked in the door, I headed straight to my room to put my book bag away. Returning to the living room, I heard Ma say something while in the kitchen cleaning the dishes.

"What's that Ma?" I yelled from the back room.

"Your brother is here," she yelled out to me from the kitchen.

"Is Benjamin home?" I asked as I entered the kitchen.

"No, Douglas," she said.

I stopped dead in my tracks. My heart almost stopped. I had been deceiving myself, thinking that he'd never return. Ma explained that he came back to New York after leaving his family and job as a prison guard. He had explained to Ma that he was attacked and stabbed by a prisoner several times and was in the hospital for the past three months. The situation had ruined his marriage.

"You just missed him, " Ma said.

"Where is he," I asked.

"He went to retrieve some of his belongings from the back of his car," she said.

I had put Douglas and what he taught me out of my life and did not wish to revisit it. Ma's Christian teachings said that the behavior was wrong and I learned to despise myself for engaging in it in the past. When Douglas arrived that afternoon I stayed clear of him. Most of the time I locked myself in my room, only leaving it to go to the bathroom or get something to eat. The time in my room was spent daydreaming about the life that I wanted, away from Douglas.

The more my life seemed to be improving, the more it felt like it was getting out of control. Lonely and having no one to talk to, I took a walk around Bronxville and found a little sparrow by a bush. The bird was squawking and as I got closer, it hopped away. I followed the sparrow and saw that it could not fly. Its wings were not fully developed. Then and there I decided to take the bird back to the apartment and take care of it.

After catching the bird between my hands, I quickly went back upstairs and looked for an empty shoebox to put it in. I found one and poked holes in its top with a sharpened pencil so the bird could breath. The bird seemed hungry so I dipped small pieces of plain white bread in water, and fed it to the bird. Wanting to know if it was a male or female, I held its beak between my fingers and pulled on it gently. The bird did not resist which told me that it was a female. If you pull on the beak of a male bird, it will put up a fight. Female birds accept their situations more easily.

Like a male bird I did not easily accept the situation I was now in. The sparrow helped me deal with the situation and brought joy into my life. She was a very musical sparrow. As she hopped around she chirped and chirped, mainly when I fed her. My love for the sparrow grew rapidly.

One afternoon I went down stairs to check the mail. Not wanting to keep the sparrow locked in the shoebox, I took my plastic laundry basket and emptied it in the corner of the room. Then I took the bird out of the box and turned the laundry basket upside down over her. Not having any money or time to buy a birdcage, I thought this will do and left. Upon my return I went into my room to check on the sparrow.

There she lay taking deep breaths. She was no longer hopping around, something was wrong. Lifting the basket with one hand, I reached under with the other and picked her up. As I held her in my hands she took a few breaths, then a long final one and then she stopped breathing. It was not meant for me to keep the bird. She belonged to the wild.

A strange sensation rose up within me. It was like I was able to feel the bird's soul leave her body. After that final breath, and feeling the strange sensation, tears fell down my cheeks. She was gone.

The right thing for me to do was to give her a proper burial. Ma collected plastic containers from old orders of wonton soup, so I took one of them and laid a piece of cloth in the container to create a casket. The sparrow was gently laid upon the cloth then sealed in the container with its plastic lid. I returned to where I first spotted the sparrow, took a stick and dug a hole in the ground beside the bush. When the hole was deep enough, I placed the makeshift casket inside it, covered it with dirt, and said a brief prayer, and then returned to my room.

Lying on the bed, I contemplated life and thought about how the sounds of sparrows once helped me keep going and not commit suicide. The sparrows will not comfort me anymore, I thought to myself, since I caused the death of one of their own. Thinking that I had to get away, I remembered seeing a flyer on the school wall. It was a flyer for dance classes after school. I returned to the spot where I had seen the flyer while at school the following day. The flyer was still on the wall. I jotted down the date and time of the class. This will be my escape from the abuse, I thought to myself.

Wanting the abuse to end but too afraid to say anything about it, I did not know to whom to turn. Remembering how my system of escape helped when I was in public school, I thought the dance classes would keep me out of the house. Basketball was another option, but my body was too frail to be on the court. So I started taking dance classes.

* * * *

One night I came home from dance rehearsal not having eaten all day. As soon as I got home I ate dinner and took a shower. My homework was done in between rehearsals, so I went directly to bed. I was so drained that night that the idea of Douglas staying with us did not faze me, besides he did not bother me since he arrived. That night he did not get home from work early so I thought I'd get some sleep.

No sooner did I fall off to sleep I was abruptly woken up by my brother forcing himself on me as I lay sleeping. With disgust I quickly jumped up out of the bed and ran into the bathroom across the hall. Feeling beaten and full of disgust, I squeezed an inch of toothpaste on my toothbrush and washed out my mouth, not forgetting to brush my tongue. After I finished washing out my mouth, I shut off the light and headed into the living room.

There sat Pa watching the Yankees playing the Oakland A's. I wanted so much to tell him what just happened in the next room, but I didn't. After all these years we still were not communicating. Ma, who mediated between us, was in her bedroom. I turned around and headed to the back room. As I approached my parent's bedroom I heard light snoring coming from the room. Ma's head was propped up by her arm, facing the television on her nightstand. The reflection of the television lit her upper body.

"Ma, are you up?" I asked but there was no response.

"Ma are you sleeping?" I tried again with no response.

I walked closer to her as her snoring got louder. There she lay sleeping and I decided it was best if I did not wake her. She had been diagnosed with hardening of the arteries and was taking nitroglycerine and wearing a patch on her chest. I thought telling her what just happened would surely put her in cardiac arrest.

Standing there for a few moments as an old re-run of *Barretta* starring Robert Blake started up again after a commercial break, I leaned toward my mother as she slept, wanting to crawl in front of her as I did when I was a child so she would protect me as she did years ago. Suddenly she took a deep breath and opened her eyes.

"Michael?" she asked.

"Yes, Ma," I said.

"What are you doing?" she asked.

"You were sleeping so I was turning off your TV," I said as I reached to the power button of the TV.

"Oh, you better get some sleep, it's getting late and you have school in the morning," she said.

"I know, Ma, I'll see you tomorrow," I said.

"If the Lord is willing," she said.

"Good night," I said as I turned around and left her room.

Having no one to talk to and nowhere to turn, I went back to my room where Douglas slept, opened the door quietly and headed straight for my bed up against the window. Quickly slipping under the covers, I covered my head with the sheet and cried myself to sleep. As the tears ran down my check, I faced the window, trying to keep my mouth shut as I gripped the pillow against my face and cried into it. I did not want Douglas to hear me. In my ears the pressure built up and the sounds of loud screams echoed through my head. I was not going to let him know the pain I was in. I accepted my situation like a female sparrow.

I occupied every moment of my time with studying and dancing while keeping it all in. My mind was forced to open itself to what was being taught in school during the day. When I had any time between classes, it was used to study class notes or read the chapters assigned in my textbooks. My English teacher assigned William Blake's *Songs of Experience and Innocence* which I read during the hours after school, and I rehearsed the choreography I was learning in my dance classes. My dance instructor informed me at the time that she was holding auditions for students to become members of a dance company in East Harlem.

The dance company was the first to be funded by a school district and the board of education and gave students the opportunity to use their talents in a professional way. A few days after the audition a sheet of paper was posted outside the dance studio listing the students who had made it into the company. My name was on the list. My love for dance grew strong, but it was my desire to get out of the apartment that motivated me. I took dance classes beginning in 1984 and from that period on the grades on my high school transcript showed improvement.

My grades improved so much that I made the honor role a couple of semesters. The academic achievements were a result of hard work and a reflection of what my soul had become. I felt golden. The glow I gave off also showed in my dancing abilities. The dance company traveled around the city performing at different school functions and cultural events. During Puerto Rican heritage month the company performed at the World Trade Center. The title of the dance was *Oye Como Va* and we danced to the song of the same name by Carlos Santana.

On another cultural holiday the company boarded a bus and went to Albany, New York where we danced on stage between two of George Rickey's sculptures that moved in the wind. Every year since the dance company was created, I worked hard so that I would be chosen to perform in the company's major dance concert at Aaron Davis Hall at the City College of New York. My favorite dance was called

Flight. It was about a mother bird protecting her young from leaving the nest. This dance was symbolic for what was happening in my mind.

It was during this time that I began constructing thoughts around what I read or around the movements of the dances I was in, to escape from reality. Escaping from reality began the day I thought sparrows were talking to me, the day I tried to kill myself. Having fleeting thoughts was damaging my psyche though it was how I survived. Taking flight in my mind also took me away from thinking about the abuse and about my developing sexuality.

Knowing that I was attracted to men made it difficult to be a part of an institution that did not acknowledge or discuss such things. Through high school there were very few people that I considered my friends. My dance partner and I were close but I mainly spent time with another girl in school who helped save me until our relationship became romantic. One morning I decided to be her boyfriend and by the afternoon I had changed my mind. By my senior year in high school I was a loner, who had to once again start looking for a way to escape my situation. The only option available to me was to apply to college.

The college advisor at MSSM set up an appointment for me to meet the Director of the Educational Opportunity Program (EOP) at Manhattanville College. Pa drove me up to Manhattanville in the fall of 1985. It was a snowy day. The cold air made me alert.

When I entered the Humanities Building I took a left and entered a long hallway. Next I walked passed the Bursar, the Registrar and then the Office of Institutional Research, the last two of which I would work eventually in during my senior year in college to satisfy the work-study requirements of financial aid. The EOP office was beyond these offices in a cul de sac.

The director showed me into his office.

"What are your carrer goals?" he asked me.

"I want to be a chemical engineer, " I said.

After about an hour the interview was over. He escorted me out the door.

"You will be notified by your college advisor," he said as he shook my hand.

"Thank you for your time," I said and left for the car that was waiting for me. Pa did not say anything to me the whole trip.

There were other colleges that I was interested in but after the meeting Manhattanville became my first choice. Besides, I never took it upon myself to send out the other applications I filled out for Skidmore and SUNY-Brockport.

When I learned about Manhattanville, I knew it was the place for me. It was a college that specialized in the liberal arts and sciences, and it allowed me to continue dancing and study chemistry. It was the ideal institution for me. Additional information about the school was sent to me in the mail.

I received information about the course offerings and a special pre-college summer program that the EOP offered to help incoming freshmen adjust to college life and get ahead in their academic studies. At the time my only thought was to graduate and attend the pre-college summer program, since it would give me the opportunity to get out of my family situation sooner than I planned.

I was successful in staying out of Douglas' way until one afternoon before graduation, when I returned to the apartment from dance class. Not feeling well, I went to lay down in the back room where Ma attempted to strangle us the first night we moved in. It had been Hannah's room when we moved in but she married and moved out of state so I took over the room. I turned on the television to relax.

As I was dosing off to sleep, I heard someone come into the room. It was Douglas, home from working as a security guard in a large Manhattan hotel. It was about three in the afternoon and everyone was coming home from school. Flora, Melissa and Jerome were finishing their last days of school. They had the same routine each day, each one dropped off their book bags in their rooms, then headed to the dining room to eat dinner.

While everyone was in the dining room, Douglas pulled the covers off my body and pulled my underwear down to my hips as usual. The routine was old hat. Starting to disrobe, he took of his shirt, leaving on his v-neck tee shirt. He then opened his pants, leaned over the bed and was about to mount me when there was a knock on the bedroom door as it opened.

"What the hell are you doing?" Ma screamed.

She was on her way back to the kitchen after stopping into her bedroom next door to get some money to send Jerome to the store for a gallon of milk. She thought to check on me, knowing that I was not feeling well.

"Nothing," Douglas said as he jumped off me. Finally, he was caught in the act and unfortunately it had to be with me. I began to rise from the bed as if I was in a deep sleep.

"You let him do that to you?" Ma yelled at me.

"What are you talking about?" I said as I raised my head from my pillow and wiped my eyes pretending to wake up from a deep sleep.

"Get your stuff and get the hell out of this apartment," she said to Douglas.

"Ma, I was just climbing off the bed," Douglas yelled back at her trying to rationalize what she saw.

The situation began to escalate, with Douglas persisting in his explanation. When my mother insisted that he leave, Douglas pulled out a gun and pointed it at her.

"I'll kill you," he said to Ma.

Uriel and Ruth ran to the back room as they heard the yelling, saw Douglas pointing the gun at Ma and grabbed him. They pushed him towards the door of the apartment, scuffling back and forth screaming.

"Let me go, I'm going," he told them.

"Get the hell out of here," Uriel said.

"Don't come back," said Ruth.

He quickly passed Ma and came back into the bedroom to grab his belongings and left.

"Are you alright," Uriel said to Ma.

"The devil is always working," Ma said as she left my room, not saying a word to me, and went into the kitchen. It was finally over, I thought to myself, he was now gone. Flora and Melissa came running back in to my room thirty minutes later.

"Michael, are you alright?" Flora asked.

"I'm OK," I said.

"Ma said Douglas tried to get fresh with you while you were sleeping," she said.

"I know that's what Ma told me," I said denying what I knew.

"I hate Douglas," said Melissa who was standing in the doorway.

"I hate him too," I said.

Three weeks later I felt the anger building up in me. All I had worked for was now gone. My soul was once again tarnished. Those first words out of Ma's mouth infuriated me as I thought about them over and over again.

"You let him do that to you?" I heard her voice repeating in my head over and over again.

Yes, it was my fault from the first day. I let it happen. As far back as the age of five, I grew and learned to desire it. Yes, I was the one responsible. Not you, Ma! I know grandma died when I was born but that is no excuse; you could have protected me.

Why was it that Ma went out of her way to protect and take care of my relatives when they stayed over but she did not protect me? Did the situation with Douglas three weeks earlier open up her eyes, I asked myself? My cousin Colin was staying with us for a couple of weeks after Douglas pulled the gun on her. Just the sight of him disgusted me, especially when I saw her caring and protecting him.

Ma ran through the same routine that she did for all her children, but there seemed to be something slightly different. She was doing more for him than she did for her own children. Her interaction with my cousin was not cold and mechanical like it was with her own flesh and blood. Maybe it was because we were in the midst of her care that I did not feel the effects of her gentle touch, or did not feel a sense of warmth and caring when she took Benjamin and me out of the tub and dressed us when we were younger.

She had been doing it so long with us that it seemed like it was mechanistic and lacked emotion. I asked myself, why on earth did she care more about my relatives that she did me? Ma was no longer drinking, so maybe she now realized how precious life was, especially the lives of children.

Now a Christian, children were little angels to her. At the time I was too old to be feeling abandoned, alone, angry and jealous but mentally I was immature. My expectations of myself were high and the fact that I was abused and had to deal with it did not make my situation any better. Taking care of my own needs was my own responsibility–this is what my alcoholic mother had taught. All that ran through my mind were the endless nights of abuse that I experienced since I was a child.

* * * *

Over and over again the abuse played in my head one afternoon as I ironed freshly washed clothes on the old circular rotating ironing machine in the back room–the same room my where mother tried to kill me and where my brother took his final mounting–was filled with the smell of Bold laundry detergent. Everyone was in the living room of the apartment. Colin walked in.

"You ironing Michael?" he asked.

"Yeah," I said as I grabbed him.

"What's the matter?" he said

"Shut up!" I replied.

"Why are you hitting me," he said.

"Shut up!" I said and beat him as he began to cry.

"Stop!" he screamed as I muffled his mouth.

"I'll kill you!" were my final words to him, the same words Douglas told Ma a few weeks prior.

When I was done he left the room and tried to tell my mother, but his cries fell on deaf ears. Douglas was in me, just like the day I saw Levi in my place as I searched my brother's pants for a few cents, or was my soul defective? I did not believe what I had just done.

"No," I kept telling myself, it was I. My soul was no longer gold, silver or bronze; it was corroding, it was dark, it was evil. The evil that was in Douglas was now in me. Just like my brother I was evil, evil, evil!

When I engaged in the abuse I did not feel myself. The only way to describe the situation is to say that I was alone with the devil and in the presence of evil. I can only describe the hollow sensation I did feel. It was like something entered my body for the moment. Colin was too young to understand what was happening to him or what my behavior towards him was all about–I myself did not know–was I too a fallen angel?

Not feeling safe at home or in my own skin, I had to find a place to save myself. I needed to get away, and college was the perfect opportunity to find out who I was and why my behavior had become like my brothers'. In early February, the college advisor told me that I was accepted into Manhattanville College and in May I received acceptance into the pre-college summer program.

When graduation came, my name was called to receive a gold plated statue for my achievements in dance. This is what my soul had become. Having gone through the refining system of the New York City Board of Education's requirements, and having struggled to achieve something, my exterior was buffed and polished but my interior was *not* golden. In June 1986 I packed my bags and headed for Manhattanville.

Chapter VIII:
A Spiritual Universe

The first summer I spent at Manhattanville was an experience of soul searching. Finding my voice was not an easy task after all I had been through. The program supplied me with free housing, food, and a stipend for books and additional expenses. Campus living resembled the ideal type of life I imagined. Everything needed was put into place.

All I had to do was attend classes, keep a good grade point average and the federal government financed my existence. The government did not ask for anything in return, and since my parents were poor, the government paid for everything. I did not need any loans. By the government investing in the education of poverty stricken individuals, it monitored students' progress and collected data by the Office of Institutional Research. In the end the government was benefiting from its investment.

Today, this sort of funding is more limited. Government aid is available to pay for tuition but not much is in the budget for housing and living expenses. This is such a disadvantage for those students who are experiencing an abusive family life and use school as a safe haven. The government no longer finances the opportunity for a child in need to relocate from a horrible home life. This opportunity and additional funding helped save my life.

My life might have ended in suicide if this outlet had not existed for me. The second time around I would not have stopped myself, and the razor would have sliced into the vein moving up along my arm. I had it all planned out and this was my method of choice. Choosing to attend Manhattanville was a life saving decision. The experience was spiritual.

The first summer I spent at the pre-college summer program at Manhattanville, I studied to improve my academic skills while in class and learned about my sexuality during the time I spent outside of the classroom. There were about twenty students participating in the program. There was one girl in the program named Jennifer who took particular interest in me.

Jennifer and I began to spend a lot of time together. Eventually the topic of sex came up and within a few weeks she pushed herself on me and I felt pressured to have sex with her one afternoon while on a break between classes. This was my first experience with a woman. Since my past was behind me, I had the opportunity to start over fresh and new.

My feelings about our sexual interaction were neutral. Even though I had put the past behind me I found it difficult to escape from the idea that sex was something I reacted to mechanically, especially given the fact the present situation involved a woman. I continued to have sex with Jennifer but did not attribute any emotion to our unions. It was not a matter of sexual pleasure that propelled me, just the desire to get the release of stress that goes with such behavior.

Trying to understand myself and fit into the socially acceptable role that was expected of me, I went along with the situation, hoping to become like my brother Benjamin who was planning to get married soon. Benjamin was just like the other guys in the program who I thought were "normal." When the other guys in the program found out about my relationship with Jennifer, I felt like a lion that had won the pride and thought I might live this type of life style.

My family was proud of me when I returned home from the summer program. Though I was the second high school graduate after Hannah, I was the first to go off to college. While at home after the summer program, I was treated with a lot of respect by my family. At home I spent most of my time reading books. One book in particular I fell in love with was the play *Equus* by Peter Shaffer.

Like Alan, the main character in *Equus*, I was experiencing major guilt. Guilt not from blinding horses, but from attempting to find out what my father had between his legs. This situation resulted in the practically non-existent relationship between my father and me. Just as in the play, my father was the cause of my shame and lack of self-esteem. Pa idolized horses and rejected his own son.

Seeing in his eyes the pleasure horses brought him while I was a young child as we stood in the horses circle the times he brought me to the race track, I pretended that I was a horse so that I too could get my father's affection. Even though Pa knew I was in a relationship with Jennifer, this was not enough to convince him that I was a man just like him and that there was no need to fear me. Thinking about my relationship with my father and the possibility of my brother Douglas returning from prison any day, I wanted to get back to Manhattanville as soon as possible.

Yes, prison. The day had finally come when the secret became known outside the immediate family. Immediately after being arrested, Douglas called Eva and explained his version of the story. He said that he was caught at his job at the hotel for stealing. Eva then called Ma with a date they were to go to the courtroom to see him.

Ma was very reluctant to go, but she went. The day Eva arrived to pick-up Ma, I developed a resentment for her. She spoke of Douglas as if he were innocent. Eva was naïve. He had lied to her about the reason for his incarceration. She was surprised when Douglas's ex-girlfriend explained to her outside the courtroom what he was actually put in jail for. She explained to them that he had tried to sexually abuse her daughters a number of times. His formal charges were sexual abuse of a minor and attempted rape, both in the first degree.

When Ma explained the story to me, I did not want to hear it, though I was relieved he was in prison. In my mind it was not over. Feeling that I was becoming just like him the day I hurt Colin, there was a struggle in me I tried to forget. Moving on with life I tried to shut my mind to the past and live a new life, starting at Manhattanville.

It was September 9, 1986 and I had to head back up to Westchester County. I was happier back at Manhattanville but I missed my family. Douglas wrote Ma from prison and inquired about my whereabouts. Ma later told me he was trying to get her to give him the telephone number to my dorm room. She never gave it to him, thank God.

While Douglas was away he called to find out how we were doing and what my brothers and sisters were up to. His true motivation was unknown and I was too frightened to find out, being on campus alone without my family to protect me if he tried to come after me. I developed a strong fear. I believed he was going to come after me and kill me if I told on him; but now it was too late, everyone knew.

Working as a prison guard, he saw first hand what happens to people who engage in the type of behavior he did with my brothers and sisters. I knew what it was like to live with the fear of people knowing the secret I kept. It was ironic that he once held the job of keeping criminals like himself in check. From what I had learned, it was now a question of how to keep my mind in check so I would not perpetuate the abuse. He was a mastermind who covered up a trail of abuse.

There was more to Douglas's story. He left Colorado and the family he developed there for a reason. One can only speculate but I strongly suspect that his wife caught him abusing their son. Ma did tell me that she had the feeling Douglas was run out of Colorado by his father-in-law, but that is the only information she shared. Did Ma know more than she shared? I think she was in denial even though she knew the truth.

One afternoon while returning from Pete's store on the corner, Ma caught Douglas trying to attack Hannah. Hannah was a toddler when it happened; it was years ago so she had to know. Ma received a phone call that brought the reality of the situation to the forefront while I was away at college. Douglas's ex-girlfriend called Ma and explained to her that he was arrested. The criminal justice system had finally caught up with him and weeded out of society the cause of a festering sore.

During my freshman year at Manhattanville there were many surprises waiting for me. Jennifer had an entourage of friends who she had met on the first few days back and told them I was her lover. Most of her new friends were gay or hung around the Gay and Lesbian Bisexual Union (GLBU).

The T-for-transgender was not added to the union until my third year. Jennifer introduced me to her new friends with whom we often had lunch or dinner with between and after classes.

My internalized homophobia made me very uncomfortable around our new gay friends, especially when they spoke of sex, which was an everyday topic of conversation. That first semester Jennifer pushed me to get to know her friends. She thought by us attending the GLBU meetings, it would give off the impression that I accepted them, so I attended a few of the meetings. One meeting I attended consisted of a topic discussion then the showing of the film, *Kiss of the Spider Woman*, based on the book by Manuel Puig.

After the meeting we all went to the campus pub for drinks. I enjoyed the experience more than I led them to believe. They had no idea of my sexual past. Jennifer became very close with one woman who attended the GLBU meetings and lived off campus with her girl friend. The couple was having problems with their relationship and Jennifer decided to comfort her while she separated from her girl friend.

I was jealous of the fact that Jennifer decided to spend time off campus one night with her new female friend in need. It was not jealousy of her being with another woman, but jealousy of the fact that she was sexually liberated and I was not. Thinking that two could play the same game, I set out to be as liberated as she was. Subconsciously, I was using her as a beard to hide my own sexual desires but my plan backfired when she exclaimed she was bisexual.

Since Jennifer no longer shielded me, I isolated and spent more time on my studies, which had begun to suffer as I became more of a social bee. Toward the end of the semester Jennifer had totally given up on her studies and knew that she was going to be academically dismissed from the university. Wanting to drag me down and out with her, she surprised me as we sat outside the nurse's office.

"Are you OK? Your roommate told me you were here," I asked.

"No Michael, I'm pregnant, I missed my period," she said.

"Are you sure?" I asked.

"Yes and the baby is yours," she said.

"Did you take a pregnancy test?" I asked.

"Not yet," she said.

"Then how do you know you're pregnant?" I asked impatiently.

"Because a woman knows when she is," she said.

She went into the nurse's office and took the pregnancy test after I insisted. Within minutes we had the results. The test was negative. After the truth came out I kept my distance from her.

Avoiding her was easy because she was indeed dismissed from the university as warned. Jennifer appealed the decision but the appeal was denied because of her grades. Her grades reflected that she did not try to do any work. This news brought me a sense of relief.

My grades were poor but I kept the required 2.0 grade point average that was required to remain a student and receive financial aid. Being able to remain at the university was a sign to me that I had better focus on my studies when I returned.

The first semester at Manhattanville was also a mind opening experience for other reasons. A world was revealed to me that I never knew existed. There were students from all over the world who attended the college. My first roommate

Ari was from Jamaica, and I learned later on in the semester that he was supplying the entire campus with drugs.

One Sunday evening I returned to campus from a weekend in the Bronx to find the light on the side of my dorm room blown out. I retrieved a bulb from the resident assistant. My dorm room was dark. Turning on my desk lamp as I entered the room I placed the light bulb in the floor lamp and noticed that there were marijuana seeds inside the base of the lamp that holds the bulb. Not thinking anything of it I walked over to my television to turn it on and it did not work.

I turned the television to see if it was plugged in and the back of the television fell off. The television was plugged in but the screws that held the back of the set on were loosened. I looked inside the back of the set to see if anything was wrong. Looking closely, I could see melted plastic on the circuit board and marijuana seeds scattered throughout the television set.

"What the hell happened here?" I asked myself.

Since the television did not work I tried to put on my stereo to listen to some music. When I tried playing *Father & Son,* my favorite Cat Stevens song, no sound came out of the right speaker of my stereo. Apparently my roommate spliced my speaker wires to connect it to his turntables. Most of my electronics were destroyed with the exception of the electric typewriter. These violations did not upset me since I had been violated worse in the past. These were just material objects. Shrugging off my roommate's behavior, I gave Ari another chance and stayed roommates with him for another semester.

The second semester became a nightmare. Ari increased his business by changing his product. He went from selling marijuana to selling crack cocaine. As I tried to sleep at night there was always someone knocking on the door for supplies. Boom! Boom! Boom!

"Who is it?" I asked.

"Is Ari in?" a voice behind the door asked.

"No! He's in the library," I yelled. Five minutes latter there was another knock on the door. Boom! Boom! Boom!

"Yeah, who is it?" I asked.

"Ari in?" another unrecognizable voice at the door asked.

"No! He's in the library," I yelled.

One afternoon I returned from chemistry class and as I walked through the door to my room, Ari's supplier was in there with him arguing with a buyer. Bob Marley's song *Exodus* was blaring out of his stereo system that was composed of different electronic pieces.

"Hey man I want my money," Ari told the young frail looking student.

"I'll have it for you next week," the student said.

"No I want it today!" Ari yelled at him.

They had given the student credit and wanted to get paid what was owed them. The student had come to the room hoping to get another hit on credit. Ari continued to demand his money and pushed the student onto my bed. His partner then reached over to my desk, pulled out my pen with the letter opener at the other end of it and held the tip of the letter opener to the student's throat.

My heart began to beat very quickly as sweat poured from the pit of my arm. As I stood in the doorway shocked by what was happening before my eyes, the student pushed Ari's partner as he arose from the bed and ran past me. Ari and his partner followed right behind him. First my roommate, then his partner, charged at me with the sharp instrument in his hand. At that moment I decided to get a new roommate. It was the end of the academic year and time to pick new room assignments anyway. By the end of my first year I had only earned twenty credits, so my chance to have a single room of my own were very slim.

* * * *

After my first academic year was completed I returned home for the summer of 1987. It was nice to be home and have the opportunity to share my college experience with my family. Life at home finally felt safe. Douglas was incarcerated for a long period of time and was no longer around. I felt calm and at peace knowing I had put the past behind me. But whenever I felt like life was going great for me it seemed that something always went awry. As I sat at the dining room table one afternoon I heard a knock on the apartment door.

"Who is it?" I asked.

"Hello," Eva said as she walked in. I immediately knew something was wrong by the tone of her voice.

"Where's Ma?" Eva asked, then headed for the master bedroom.

Within a matter of minutes I heard Ma and Eva shouting at one another. It was unclear what they were arguing about.

"He got fresh with me," Eva said to Ma.

"Why are you dredging up the past," Ma said.

"Why won't you believe me," Eva said.

We all knew that Eva was having a lot of health problems, but what they were discussing had to do with something that happened years ago. As they argued I sat at the table holding my head and trying to figure out the pieces of information

I heard. It must have been what Eva was going through personally that prompted her to dredge up the past.

Eva was suffering from cancer, not to mention that she was the one Douglas went to when he got arrested. The past few months had been very stressful for her. Something was bothering her and prompted her to come all the way from Long Island to the Bronx to argue with Ma. As I sat at the table trying to listen Uriel returned from walking Taxi. She heard the screaming from the back room.

"What is going on?" Uriel asked.

"Eva is inside arguing with Ma about something," I said.

"Why won't you believe me," Eva yelled.

Eva then walk into the living room and headed for the door. Before she left the apartment she mumbled something incomprehensible to Uriel and me and then walked out letting the door slam behind her. Uriel and I ran to Ma's room to find out what the confrontation was all about.

Ma was sitting on her bed with the edges of her mouth in a frown and eyebrows drooping.

"Eva came to tell me that your father made sexual advances at her when she was a child," Ma said.

In her explanation she never made it clear whether or not Pa had sexually abused her. Hearing this made my head begin to spin.

"My God! Was it Pa all along? " I said to myself.

All this time I believed that the sexual abuse started as a result of Douglas being abused in St. Joseph's and then passing the virus of abuse to my family. At that moment I really had to get to the root of the problem, so I listened to what Ma had to say about the situation.

"When Eva was a young girl she had accused Pa of getting fresh with her. When I confronted your father about the situation he denied the accusations," she said.

"But why did Eva come back some twenty years later and accuse Pa again?" I asked.

"I don't know," Ma said.

"It's not true, Pa never touched any of the children, besides, he was always out of the house with his friends," I said.

"When Eva initially accused Pa, she was living with us, since Mount Loretta called me to come and get her because she was causing trouble for everyone," Ma said.

Eva was now showing symptoms of a borderline personality disorder, and was going out of her way to wreak havoc. I think that Eva accused Pa as a result of jealousy.

"She was jealous of the fact that Ma had created a family with Pa and took care of all the children," I said to Uriel as she stood beside Ma's bed.

"Eva's biological father went off to California after I was involved with him. He wanted me to go with him but I decided to stay in New York. I was pregnant with Eva at the time and never told him," Ma said.

Ma never told me the story about Eva and Pa before because she believed it was not true. Thoughts about my past abuse were now once again becoming confused and complicated in my mind by what Ma was telling me. The thought crossed my mind that it was most likely Douglas who was making sexual advances at Eva while she was asleep, but Douglas was six years younger than Eva and not around at the time. Eva's accusations pointed to Pa as the initial source.

The earliest memory of my abuse left me with a phantom. That morning I never saw who left my room. Was it Pa who preyed on me that morning? Until now I believed my desire to know was a result of the games that Douglas played with me. I could not bring my self to believe that Pa was the root of the evil. All the physical evidence pointed to Douglas. If only I had that cotton T-shirt today, a DNA analysis would help me know. I had to find out the truth, but I needed help. When I returned for my sophomore year at college, I registered for a philosophy class, thinking I'd be able to figure out the truth.

Between 1987 and 1988, my second year at Manhattanville, I shared my room with two different students. The first was an African-American ladies man. He was hardly ever in the room. One day I dared to ask him where he spent his time when he was not in the room.

"Hanging out with the ladies," he said.

My third roommate was a Frenchman who constantly talked about dating a famous French actress.

"My girl friend was a French film star," he said.

"What movies has she made?" I asked.

"She starred in the French film titled *Paulina à la Plage*, he said.

"I never saw it," I said.

"There is a copy of it in the library, see it if you have time," he encouraged.

"Are you still seeing her?" I asked.

"We separated after my accident," he said.

The accident left him physically challenged. With his disability, he spent plenty of time in our dorm room reading. Both of my roommates moved out mid semester so I had a double sized room the majority of that year. Having a single room contributed to my academic dismissal my second year at Manhattanville.

Feeling sexually liberated with Jennifer no longer on campus and a group of gay friends she left behind, I explored relationships with men trying to determine my ultimate preference. This was much different than just having sex. That semester I met a guy named Robert who was a transfer student from S.U.N.Y-New Paltz. The more time I spent with him the more I got to know him. He was so nice to me and extremely handsome. Falling in love with him, I easily gave myself to him physically.

It was a giant step for me to get involved with someone who was considered "out of the closet." I myself was closeted. But thinking I found the person I was going to spend the rest of my life with, I came out. In time everyone on campus knew my secret; and I believed my secret was safe because it was not known in the Bronx. But, I was not the only one with a secret. When I became intimate with my new lover, I discovered what I had no idea even existed.

"Robert, your penis is so small," I said as I touched him below.

"Is that a problem?" he asked.

"No," I said.

A few seconds later I had another burning question I needed to ask.

"Robert, why is your anus right below you penis?" I asked.

"That's not my anus," he said.

"What do you mean?" I asked.

"I am male and female," he said.

Robert was a he and a she. Robert explained he was a hermaphrodite. I did not know about the intersexed. I accepted my lover and followed his lead when it came to what was done in bed. It was like having sex with Andrew and his twin sister at once.

I walked around campus with my head held high with a newfound pride, defying Ma's Christian teachings. This feeling did not last after I learned that Robert had another boyfriend on the other side of the campus where the student apartments were. Living in the dorms, I had no clue about Robert's double life. Sadly, after having sex with me he ignored me. I was just another notch in his belt, fresh meat to him that was now tainted. Obviously he did not know my past, or that I was not uncharted territory.

Having fallen in love with Robert, I felt soul loss when he abandoned me. As I sat in my dorm room staring in disbelief when he ignored my calls, I felt my soul rise above me just as the day the little sparrow died in my hand. This was the second out of body experience I felt where a spirit rose above me. Also feeling rejected I retreated back into the closet and became involved with a woman named Cathy. I easily fell in love with her as she comforted me as I explained how I was used and rejected. She was also convenient in helping me attempt, once again, to hide my true sexuality.

Even though I loved her, I still desired men. By the end of my second year in college I was up for academic dismissal, but successfully appealed and was given a second chance to complete my degree. Cathy on the other hand was unable to afford the university and had to move back to New York City and attend a community college.

In my third year at Manhattanville academia once again became a priority and relationships became second. Even though Cathy was now living off campus, she came up from New York City from time to time to visit. When she was not on campus I suppressed the desires I had for men. My soul was torn between both men and women when I realized that I was in love with Cathy. The mental ambivalence was becoming physical.

One night, during a weekend she stayed with me on campus, we made passionate love and fell asleep. In the middle of the night I woke up roaring like a lion. It was an evil roar. I was fighting my inner desires trying to make the relationship work. The relationship did not last. Not only because it was a long distance relationship, but also because I began sleeping with a man I knew since high school. Learning from what Robert did to me, I too juggled two relationships, until Cathy learned about it. I no longer was able to live with the deception.

Throughout my college career I bounced in and out of relationships with men and women trying to figure out who I was. By my fourth year in college men had become my first choice. The sexual abuse I had experienced as a child confused me so much that when I became an adult I was still unsure what to do with myself. I thought that if sexuality is biologically determined, my experiences as a child created a form of defect.

I became even more confused one afternoon while I was walking across campus to my dorm after lunch. Clouds gathered over me as I noticed a tall elderly man walking towards me. He was dressed in a pair of dark brown slacks and a wool blazer. He looked very distinguished with white hair combed to the side and full white beard and mustache. I seemed to recognize his face. The sky became cloudy as I noticed my old English teacher from high school about to pass me. He suddenly stopped beside me.

"Hi, Michael, how are you?" he asked.

"I'm fine, how about you?" I asked.

"Doing well," he said.

After some awkward silence he asked me in a very nervous tone of voice.

"Would you like to play with some children I know tonight?" he asked.

"What do you mean?" I asked.

"I mind some children, would you like to come along and play with us tonight?" he asked.

"I really can't I have to study for an exam," I said.

"Maybe next time," he said. It started to rain heavy.

I have to go, see you around campus," I said as I walked away.

After leaving him all I thought about was an old man playing sexual games with little children and I wondered why was he asking me? This was the same man who taught me William Blake's *Songs of Innocence and Experience*. Did he know something about my past? When ever I had predatorial thoughts towards children I acknowledged them for what they were and let them pass through my consciousness. It always seemed when I got my life on track there was some other force that entered to derail me.

By my fourth year in college I was back on track with a single room. It was difficult to get a single room but I had accumulated the 65 credits needed to get one. Putting all my focus and attention into my studies I completed a senior thesis and marched in June.

All the marching that Benjamin did in the Cub Scouts did not compare to the achievement I had accomplished. Once again I had the opportunity to let my golden soul shine and in my entire luster did not get the attention, let alone some communication, I desired from my father. No matter how golden I thought my soul was, it was not bright enough to earn his love.

117

Sure enough, I thought if I sought his crotch once again he'd pay attention to me. It worked in the past and led him to yell at me, a sign that he knew I existed. Some attention was better than none. Wanting male attention, I conveniently became involved in a relationship with Patrick before I graduated from Manhattanville. Patrick was a guy I met at Manhattanville through mutual friends.

Patrick graduated a year before me and visited me while I was still a student and close to graduating. He was planning to move into Manhattan from Upper Saddle River, New Jersey. The last semester at Manhattanville, I decided to withdraw from campus housing and used the refund money to move into Manhattan with him. Not wanting to return to the South Bronx after living in Westchester County for five years, a cozy apartment on Central Park West became my new address.

The refund money from my financial aid lasted for a couple of months, so this gave me time to find a job. I worked at a check-cashing place for a few weeks, but having only 119 credits after my last semester was over, I still needed one more credit to officially graduate.

Miraculously there was an ad in the *New York Times* classified section for a court clerk/process server at a top New York City law firm, so I applied for the position and got the job. It was June 1991 and I had already marched in graduation, so after accepting the job offer, I explained my situation to my new supervisor and brought her a copy of my graduation program with my name listed in it as proof. She allowed me to work the first six months as a paid internship and filled out the evaluation so that I got the additional credit that confirmed me as a September 1991 graduate.

Everything seemed to fall into place for me. Within six months I completed my degree, was promoted at my new job, and was living the type of life I daydreamed of as a child. Living a yuppie lifestyle, we mostly dined out at night, had our clothes sent to the cleaners, and traveled. Every October that Patrick and I were together we took trips abroad.

We vacationed together in Greece, Turkey, Portugal, and on the Island of Madeira. On October 21, 1993 we boarded the eastbound flight number 418 from John F. Kennedy (JFK) airport to Athens, Greece. We arrived in Athens and shuttled to the Caravel Hotel and went straight to bed to be well rested for our first day of exploration.

The first place I wanted to visit was the Acropolis. As we climbed up the path, the temple of Athena was on our right, the Cyclades on our left and a view of Zeus' temple in front of us. After visiting the museum and taking in the view we headed back down to tour the streets of Athens. That afternoon while walking in the Plaka we grabbed a gyro to fuel up.

Being familiar with the area from studying our guidebook we decided where to dine that evening. The second night in Athens we ate mousaka, a traditional Greek meal at Byzantine, a lovely restaurant in the Plaka that was nestled below the Acropolis which was beautifully illuminated at night. As I sipped on ouzo, the fact that I was in Greece hit me. I was so excited to be there that by the third day, just as the opening line in Plato's *Republic*, I too went down to Piraeus but did not stop there.

Continuing on to Vouliagmeni, I stripped nude and laid in the crevice below a cliff on the Ionic Sea. It was much more clear and beautiful than the city of Athens filled with heavy smog. That night when we got back to our hotel we felt energized and wanted to go out. We headed out around 10:30 p.m. and climbed a steep hill to my first gay dance club experience, but learned that the Club Alexander did not open up until midnight. Returning to the club when it opened, I later learned that this club had nothing on clubs in New York and Miami.

Our trip did not end in Athens. In Piraeus we boarded the MTS Arcadia and traveled to the islands of Patmos, Mykonos, Rhodes, Crete, and Santorini. During our cruise through the Greek islands we stopped in Kushadasi, Turkey, where I shopped for souvenirs and was given a free glass eye by a store merchant, to help ward off the evil eye the people in that part of the world believe exists. By the time we got back to Athens we accumulated extra luggage to carry home. On our return home we boarded a flight from Athens to JFK where we had a car waiting for us to take us back to our cozy apartment on Central Park West.

* * * *

Patrick was from a more refined background. His family was upper middle class and lived in a well maintained home in Upper Saddle River. His parents were hip baby boomers who were educators always out on the go. Every time they called the apartment his parents were off traveling to some remote destination.

One one occasion we vacationed with Patrick's parents when they rented a lovely Victorian home on the Jersey shore. When we arrived at the home, Patrick's mother realized that she forgot the set of keys that the realtor had given her. It was about dusk when the four of us arrived. Patrick decided that he and his mother would drive to the realty office about 50 minutes away to get another set of keys.

As Patrick's father and I waited he headed to the rear of the home.

"Come see the yard," he told me.

"OK," I said as I followed him through a white wooden gate at the side of house.

We walked down a long square tile path between the house and wooden fence to the back yard. Above the yard was a deck that looked out to the ocean. There was a deck above the yard attached to the house with a ramp that extended from the house to the beach.

"Isn't that a beautiful sunset," he said.

"Yeah, its very nice," I said.

"It's going to be a nice evening," he said.

"It's nice and warm," I said trying to keep up with the small talk. As the sun went down and it became darker his father became quiet and acted a bit strange.

"Some times I feel like I'm being tested," he said.

"Tested?" I asked not understanding what he was talking about.

"Yes, tested," he said with a nervous tone and then was silent.

He made me begin to feel uncomfortable. It was getting darker and he was fading before me into the darkness. There were lights under the deck above us that flickered then turned on and lit up the back yard.

"Alright," I said, as he remained silent.

Moving under the deck below the light, he moved closer to me and then I realized what he was talking about. Patrick's father was trying to conceal an erection as he drew near. This took me back to my childhood. I realized what was about to happen and did not give him the opportunity to make an advance towards me.

"It's beautiful here by the beach," I said.

"Yes, it is nice," he said.

"Have you been here before?" I asked.

"Yes, a couple of times but we rented different houses," he said.

"Did you ever stay at this particular house before?" I asked.

"No, this is our first time here," he said.

Firing one question after the other to him I tried to divert his attention from what was obviously on his mind.

"Let's wait out front," I said as I headed for the wooden gate.

He did not say anything but followed right behind me. Taking control of the situation I was able to prevent a disaster. By the time Patrick and his mother returned with the keys the topic of conversation was on Chinese poker. Patrick told me his father loved gambling, which is why they chose the Jersey shore to vacation so that they were close to Atlantic City which was their next destination after staying at the Victorian.

Soon after Patrick and I returned home from our vacation at the shore with his parents, our relationship took a turn for the worse. Patrick started staying at work late and avoided coming home after work. When he did get home at a decent time he spent the rest of the evening talking to his father on the phone both raising their voices at one another.

"What's wrong," I asked.

"Nothing, my father is being difficult," he said.

From overhearing one discussion it sounded as if his father was giving him an ultimatum, if he wanted to receive a total of thirty thousand dollars. One month later Patrick had surprising news for me that I did not see coming at all.

"I won't be here when you get home from work tomorrow, I'm moving out," he said.

"What do you mean your moving out, when did you get an apartment?" I asked.

"This week while I was at work," he said.

"OK, if that is what you want," I said in total disbelief.

I thought he must have been bluffing. We had had an argument a week before, after I explained to him what had happened with his father at the Jersey shore. Besides, he was not in any financial situation to get his own apartment let alone have enough money for a security deposit and one month's rent. Our lease was up at the end of the month and we were weeks away. Even knowing this I still didn't believe he was leaving, there was no reason for him to leave or any discussion about separating.

When I returned home from work the next day the apartment was empty except for my belongings. I was devastated. There was no bed for me to sleep on. He did not say that we were breaking up, just that by the time I returned home the next day, he'd be gone and just like that he was gone. All his belongings vanished. The only remaining items were my things. My desk, home gym, bookshelf, and clothes were piled in the corner of the living room. Not accepting what Patrick told me the night before, I was in shock. He did not shut the phone off or take it, so I called Ma.

"Ma, Patrick moved out on me," I said.

"He left?" she asked.

"Yeah, the apartment was empty when I got home," I said.

"Well, come on home," she said.

"I have too, I have nothing to sleep on, he took all the furniture with him," I said.

"You're joking," she said.

"Ma he cleaned the apartment out," I said.

"Well come on home," she said.

123

"I'll be there soon, I love you," I said.

"I love you too," she said and hung up the phone.

Ma never wanted me to move out in the first place. I hopped on the number two train at 96th Street and Broadway and headed north to the Bronx. I spent the night at Ma's and she, Benjamin, Jerome and myself returned to the apartment with a U-Hall the next day to retrieve my things. As we gathered my things I noticed a large black Hefty bag that Patrick left in the corner of the kitchen, with items he did not think worth keeping. As I looked in the garbage bag I fished in and pulled out packs of photos that were taken on our trips to different locations around the world. He threw away our memories.

To me this said that he no longer wanted them or me as part of his life, but I took the pictures with me to keep them as mine. Later on I found out that Patrick came to the apartment and saw my family and me moving out my belongings but did not interrupt us. I also learned that the real story behind our separation was that he was frequenting sex booths and discovering a new sexual freedom. One afternoon after our separation I met him for lunch at the Rocking Horse Cafe. Over coffee he explained his new found pastime and how it works.

"There is a slot at the bottom of the windows in the sex booth to insert your penis to be stroked or for a blow job," he said.

"You say there is a screen that can be opened or closed at the push of a button?" I asked.

Pushing people's buttons was something I was learning how to do.

"What about you father, Patrick?" I asked.

"What about him?" he asked.

"What we talked about before you left," I said.

"What are you talking about," he said being vague.

"The fact that your father was coming on to me with a full fledged erection," I said with my voice rising.

"My father is gay," he said.

"Gay?" I said.

"Yeah, he's queer," he said.

"What about your mother, does she know?" I asked.

"She doesn't have a clue," he said.

"That's not right," I said.

"My father and I have an arrangement," he said.

"What kind of arrangement?" I asked.

"As long as I keep quiet I get whatever I want," he said.

"You sound bought," I said.

"If the price is right," he said.

This was a side of Patrick I never knew. The more I spoke to him the more frustrated and disgusted I was getting. He diverted our conversation back to sex booths and bathhouses and I started becoming interested in learning about them for myself. I too began to frequent these places with intention to learn about men's sexual behavior. The more I went, the more I learned about myself. I learned what motivates me and what helps control the sexual predatorial thoughts I developed.

Three months later I met up again with Patrick. Our meeting was similar to the previous one, and he continued to advocate for sexual promiscuity and his new lifestyle.

"I don't know why people think it is such a big deal, it's acting on human instinct," Patrick said.

"Patrick, people are taught it is wrong to have sexual feelings for the same sex and even when a forum is provided for two men to connect sexually it is in a place that is designed to have as little human contact as possible. That is why there are separate rooms with thick glass separating you from the person you meet, so that you can feel guilty that you are doing something wrong while you're doing it," I said.

Patrick totally agreed with my explanation because it helped justify his behavior. This was not the same guy that I had met at Manhattanville College. When I met him he was a young meek Italian boy, five feet five with soft brown hair and innocent doe eyes-well spoken and very creative. He studied set design in college and started out as a paste up artist until he evolved into a full-fledged art director who was semi-independent. I say semi-independent since he never had to worry about the great amount of financial debt he got himself into. Whenever his credit cards reached beyond forty thousand dollars, his dad in Upper Saddle River received a telephone call requesting help to bail him out.

Being his only close connection in New York I was to pick up on the emotional slack that was lacking in his upper middle class family. There was a lot to Patrick's past that he did not fully discuss, and I knew from the night at the beach with his father and how easily his father responded to his requests that something was not quite right. It appeared Patrick had more information about his father than just his being gay, and that his father was afraid of other people finding out. I had a good idea what the extent of it was.

Chapter IX:
Cosmic Code/Soul of God

After moving back home to the Bronx in 1994 every moment of my life was filled with doing something. Movies, dance concerts, dinner with friends, ballroom dancing, jogging, academic classes, anything I could think of to do I did hoping to keep me out of the apartment. Douglas was no longer there so what? I asked myself what I was running from. While attending Hunter College to earn an advanced degree, I met Jason in a psychology class.

The moment I walked into the classroom I spotted his clean-shaven head and made a beeline for the seat next to his. There was chemistry when we spoke to each other. We became the best of friends. Jason helped me escape from what was on my mind.

I was attracted to Jason the first day I laid eyes on him on the first day of classes at Hunter. Since the class was extremely crowded, I left work early to get a seat in the front. Stopping in the lobby to get a coffee, I saw my literature professor from the previous semester. He had that distinguished academic look with tweed jacket and baggy khakis.

"Hi, professor," I said.

"Hi, Michael, are you taking Lit II this semester?" he asked.

"No, I was closed out of the class. I went to the class yesterday and asked Professor Long for permission but she said the class was already too large for another student," I said.

"Well maybe next semester then," he said.

"Maybe," I said.

"See you later," he said as he walked away.

"Bye," I said.

When I got to the classroom Jason was already there, I did not know who he was at the time but was easily drawn to him. There was something about having a bald head that pulled me in his direction. This was something he had in common with *Mr. Clean* that seemed to be in fashion. Strangely enough, his sexuality was unrecognizable when we met. He glanced over to me as I sat in a chair one seat away from him.

"Hi," I said.

"Hello."

"Is this Developmental Psychology?" I asked.

"Yeah," he said.

"My name is Michael," I said as I reached out to shake his hand.

"I'm Jason," he said extending his right hand.

"Nice to meet you," he said.

"Are you ready for the semester?" I asked.

"I think so, have you heard anything about this professor?" he asked.

"No, this is the first time I'm taking him," I said.

"I haven't heard anything about him either. When I checked out the books for the course in the bookstore most of them were already gone, so it seems like a lot of people are registered for the course," he said.

"Is this your first semester?" I asked.

"Yeah, I'm trying to earn enough credits to get a degree in Psychology," he said.

"Cool, I'm undecided but only have a few more classes to take before I can graduate," I said.

Our initial conversation was superficial, but we seemed to hit it off. It was nice to meet and spend time with new people after being with the same people day in and day out at the law firm, especially people as exotic as Jason.

Jason was from the Philippines. He was tall and slender. His eyes were slightly slanted and he had a naturally copper complexion. He wore a flannel shirt with the arms cut off exposing his toned arms, and faded jeans with rugged work boots. I was intimidated by his road worker look. As soon as I spotted him I was attracted to his rough exterior but I was afraid to get too close.

When he opened his mouth a soft tone exited his fully curved lips. The opposite extremes drew me in and I did not even notice that the classroom filled up until our professor walked in and dropped his brief case and textbooks on the desk in the front of the room. All the students quickly quieted down as the instructor introduced himself and went into the first lecture of the semester.

After an hour and thirty mines went by the professor stopped talking and the students began getting up from their chairs to leave the room.

"See you next Tuesday," I said in Jason's direction as I got up from my seat and headed for the door.

"Later," he responded.

129

Time went quickly that semester. It felt like class had just begun and the professor was already talking about the midterm review. I looked over to Jason and could see by the expression on his face that he was panicking. He must have felt me looking at him and turned in my direction. My pen fell out of my hand and on to the floor as I quickly turned in my chair to face the other way. We both reached to the floor at the same time to retrieve my pen. He got their first and lifted my pen off the square linoleum floor and handed it to me.

"Thank you," I said. "Are you ready?"

"Ready?" he asked.

"Yeah, to take the midterm," I said.

"I think so, why do you want to study?" he asked.

He was sexy and I wanted have the opportunity to get to know him better.

"OK," I said trying to hide my excitement.

"Do you want to meet in the Library on Tuesday before class?" I asked.

"You guys going to get together?" a female voice from behind me asked.

Jason quickly glanced at me then began looking beside his chair for his book bag. In response to his reaction I froze, still looking to the front of the classroom. We both heard her and ignored her at the same time. It was quite mean but we instinctively had the same reaction, although I was less obvious than Jason. Our classmate left after not getting a response from either of us.

"Let's meet at a coffee house on Wednesday," he suggested.

I thought that was kind of an artist type suggestion for someone who looked so butch.

"Meet me at the Coffee Pot in Hell's Kitchen on Wednesday at 6:30pm. It's near World Wide Plaza on 50th Street and 10th Avenue," he said.

We walked out of the classroom together. I usually darted out before he packed his bag, but this time I waited for him. As we exited the building I double-checked the address with him.

"See you Wednesday," I said.

"Wednesday," he said.

In my head, I began to sing an altered version of the chorus of the marriage song from Barbara Streisand's *Yental*:

Tomorrow night. Tomorrow night.

Under the canapé I'll stand with *him* tomorrow night,

And place ring upon *his* hand with *him* all dressed in white.

Tomorrow night, tomorrow night, tomorrow night is now tonight!

I arrived five minutes early, ordered a Cappuccino, and grabbed a seat at a table towards the back of the cafe facing opposite the bathroom. When Jason arrived he grabbed a coffee and joined me. We quickly got down to business running through all the theories of developmental psychology from Piaget to Freud's Oedipal and Electra complexes. Talking about the psychosexual development of children while studying for our midterm exam made it easier for us to begin talking about ourselves without specifically stating our own sexuality.

We knew each other's sexuality without having to literally say we were gay. By the time we finished studying Jason invited me to go out with him the next night.

"My apartment is a few blocks away from here, come by at around 8:30," he said as he wrote his address down on a piece of paper and handed it to me. Inside I was very excited about the prospect of going out with him. I had never been to a New York City club before.

Once we shared with each other that we were gay, our friendship became even stronger. Future studying sessions then took place at the Big Cup in the heart of Chelsea. Sure, I had lived a gay lifestyle with Patrick, but the life Jason was showing me was a whole new world.

I found his apartment number on the intercom and rang it.

"It's me, Michael," I said into the intercom.

"Come on up," he said.

I was out of breath when I reached the top of the three flights of stairs. Although I looked good my body was not in shape. Dressed in all black, I felt confident that it made me look sexy and slimmer than I was.

"Hey, you look nice," Jason told me as he opened the door.

He was not used to seeing me in casual dress clothing. Every time I went to class straight from work I had on office drag. His apartment had been gutted and renovated into a modern studio overlooking 10th Avenue. It was one long room divided with muslin fabric that hung from the ceiling on fishing string and wooden poles. The apartment definitely had an artistic touch.

Jason explained to me that he studied fine art at the Fashion Institute of Technology as he showed me painting after painting of nude males. He seemed to be obsessed with the male physique, having paper cutouts of male bodies from the *HX* and *Next* magazines all over his refrigerator.

"Want something to drink?" he asked.

"Sure, what do you have?" I asked.

"Juice, soda, water," he said.

"I'll have some soda," I said looking at his nude portraits.

"These are really good Jason, have you shown your work anywhere?" I asked.

"I had a couple of shows and sold some of my work but it is a difficult work, the most difficult part being having to separate with the art after so much time and energy goes into creating a painting or sculpture," he said.

"I can only imagine," I said, having taken on the art of writing.

My narcissistic instinct was that Jason was going to ask me to take off my clothes and model for him. Instead he asked me to have a seat on one of the two futons that filled half of the room. MTV's *The Real World* was on the television. He took a seat on the adjacent futon.

"What do you think about Puck?" he asked.

"He is kind of evil," I said.

"Evil?" he asked.

"Yeah, considering the way he treats Pedro, you know the housemate who is struggling with HIV," I said.

"He's soon to be voted out of the house," he said.

"Who, Puck or Pedro?" I asked.

"Puck, anyway we should be leaving soon," he said.

Jason showered, shaved and spent a decent amount of time getting dressed. As he went through his closet to find his outfit for the night he explained the process of dressing in drag and how much it is all an illusion. Smoke and mirrors is what dressing up is all about.

"It's a costume just to give off a particular image," he said.

"Just like Halloween," I said.

"You can say that, but it's a fiction that becomes a part of one's reality," he said.

Jason put on three different outfits and I must admit with each costume he became a different person before me. He first tried on a pair of dark pants with a white tee shirt and covered it with an opened button up silky shirt, resembling a blast from the disco past. He danced around pretending he held a partner and danced the Hustle, looking in the mirror mounted on the closed door.

"No," he said.

"No?" I asked.

"This outfit is a No!" he said.

The second costume he tried was a torn up cotton white T-shirt with a pair of ripped jeans, black combat boots and dark shades. He resembled someone from a bad 80's MTV video, a character I thought I saw in Elton John's *I'm Still Standing*. Beginning to dance like Pat Bennatar in her *Love is a Battle Field* video, I quickly interjected.

"That is a No!" I said.

"I think your right, on to the next," he said.

He finally settled on his rough construction worker costume, flannel shirt, faded blue jeans, construction boots and a cap.

"That's very Village People's *YMCA*," I said.

"Yeah, but that is what the boys like," he said.

This was the first verbal indication that he was homosexual. An hour later Jason and I left his apartment and headed for Club USA. As we approached the club I began to get a bit nervous, not knowing what to expect. The night seemed to be going well so far. The doors opened at 9:00 and if you arrived before 10:00pm the admission was free, including an open bar. Many of the club kids were really not hip to this. Most people seemed to want to arrive after the club was already jumping, spending most of the night getting ready.

"Keep your shirt open," Jason said to me as we waited in line.

The line shortened about eight people at a time. When we got up to the bouncer at the door, he clipped shut the velvet rope and Jason and I stood there trying to look desirable so they'd let us in. There were a couple of guys ahead of us the bouncers did not let in mostly because of the way they were dressed. The bouncer unclipped the rope and motioned the both of us in. We just made it. It was getting late and as we were on line a drag queen was getting the booth ready for paying customers.

Jason knew the place like the back of his hand and quickly directed me to the bar. I stopped in my tracks when I got inside the place and saw its interior. There was a huge dance floor. Off to the side was a yellow slide that twisted down from the second floor level. There were nets hanging from the ceiling and flashing lights all around. It resembled an indoor amusement park that easily converted into a water park when foam parties were held. The bartender handed Jason a Vodka Cranberry.

"I'll have a Whiskey Highball," I said remembering the name from a place mat I read at a dinner once.

"What's that you're having?" Jason asked.

"Whisky and ginger ale," said the bartender.

"Yeah, Whisky Ginger Ale" I said.

I was nervous but excited. The only club I had ever been to was Club Alexander in Athens, Greece while vacationing with Patrick. Jason was such a godsend who tried to help me get away from my relationship with Patrick. Jason did not know that as he introduced me to the club scene Patrick was introducing me to sex booths and bathhouses. During the time I saw Jason I continued to see Patrick. Whenever I tried to talk to Jason about Patrick he had the same response.

"Don't go there, Michael, " he'd say whenever I tried to talk to him about Patrick.

"I know, but we are still good friends," I said.

"Let it go," said Jason.

"Let me tell you what happened the last time I saw him," I said.

Off and on I saw Patrick and house sat for him while he was away on business. His apartment was on West 51 Street, a central location from which to get around the city and explore the seedy underworld life above a 42nd Street not yet fully cleaned up by the Gulliani administration.

"The sexual underworld is Patrick's and my newly found activity to help separate us as a couple," I told Jason.

"Let it go, Michael," he said.

When I think about it, Patrick was a bit twisted having such a strong desire to include me in his new sexual explorations.

"Just listen to what he told me the last time we got together," I said.

"There are rows of small rooms separated by windows between them with automatic shutters in between. You know like that Madonna video where she is dancing at the peep show," Patrick told me.

"Do you mean *Open Your Heart?*" I asked.

"Yeah!" Patrick said.

" I thought that video was about people running from true love and getting engulfed in a sexual addiction, " I said.

"He was so excited about the whole thing and automatically expected me to accept his behavior. Didn't he know how I must have felt thinking that he wanted to spend time with me because he loved me. His motives for contacting me after we separated was to have a buddy to share his sinful behavior that was not accepted by larger society," I told Jason.

Beginning to feel like I was a priest in a confession booth I made the decision to start keeping my distance from Patrick. Jason was right; Patrick was no good for me but nights out with Jason were not so innocent either. They both were showing me a way to get sexual pleasure but they each had their own style in doing it. Jason's approach was more refined while Patrick's was raw. The opposite approach was to be expected from each of them.

Clubbing and cruising never existed to me before Jason came along. He took me to Club USA, Roxy, Tunnel, and many other clubs and bars in New York. Jason told me that gay nightlife existed all over the world, and about his life in San Francisco and how he lived as a woman. This all fascinated me but something was missing and still not right in my life.

Deep down inside I wanted to run, to disappear, so I began to travel more. Running away from my situation did not help because I could not run from the fact that I was abused, that I perpetuated the abuse by harming my cousin, and that what I thought was my ideal relationship ended. Even though I continued to see Patrick on and off, Jason disapproved, especially when I told him how Patrick was sharing his experiences in sex booths with me. Inside I felt like my world was falling apart. Running away to Miami helped me escape from it all.

On March 3, 1995 I boarded a flight from JFK to Miami International Airport. When I arrived in Miami with Jason, we took a Super Shuttle that transferred us to the Shore Club Hotel on Collins Avenue. My plan was to stay in Miami for three days. The reason Jason and I went was to attend the Winter Party, a gay circuit party that takes place every March. Jason and I had a blast.

South Beach and the gay scene were not new to Jason but they were new to me. Jason showed me all the fun places to hang out. We went to a bunch of different bars and clubs. Jason took me to Twist, Paragon, Icon, Westend, and Club Ozone. The day after a hard night of clubbing Jason and I laid on the beach till noon then hung out at cafés sipping coffee and cruised the boys. We also cruised Ocean Drive and Lincoln Avenue.

Vacationing in South Beach helped me explore myself and become more comfortable with my sexuality. My appearance fit in well with the Maimi gay scene. Trying to look like a muscle boy, I went to the gym and lived off of vitamin supplements to maintain my weight and fit into a medium size bikini. The last day of my stay on South Beach was the highlight of my trip. The party on the beach kicked off around noon. Jason and I walked from our spot on the beach to the party. The sun was very hot that day. My skin had a bronze color to it. At the party Jason left me for a few moments to get us some drinks.

Upon his return I introduced him to a few people I had just met. There was a blond woman named Robin wrapped in a sarong talking to an African-American male with piercing green eyes. They had moved closer to where I was standing and struck up a conversation with me. As we talked, Jason approached and had a look of surprise on his face. He almost dropped the drinks he was carrying. Jason handed me my drink and pulled me over to the side.

"Do you know whom you are talking to?" he asked.

"No" I said. I really did not care because I was having fun.

"That's Robin Byrd," he said.

"Who?" I replied.

"Robin Byrd the porn star," Jason said in frustration.

"She is the one with the cable show *Men for Men*," he said.

Being clueless I just continued to talk to her and her friend. I then began to think of becoming a porn star myself. Being an exotic dancer always appealed to me, but the thought of becoming a porn star was even better. Robin's friend had a tattoo of a star on his upper arm.

"Why did you choose a star?" I asked.

"It's what I wanted," he said.

"I'm thinking about getting one myself," I said.

"You should think and pick something that you want to be with for the rest of your life," he said.

That was the end of our conversation. He went on talking with Robin about private parties that I knew nothing about.

"It was nice talking to you," I told them as I left the party with Jason.

My flight was leaving the next evening so I had to see as much of Miami Beach as I could. The night of the beach party all the clubs were having separate parties of their own, so Jason and I hopped from one club to the next. As we sat in Twist having a drink I got serious with Jason.

"Jason, you know we have known each other for a while now," I said.

"I know, what's up," he said.

"Jason, I'm attracted to you," I said.

"That's sweet Michael," he said.

"I'm also sexually attracted to you," I told him.

"Michael, you're like a sister too me," he said.

"Sister!" I said.

"Yeah," he said "You're my best friend. We're good friends, Michael. Besides it would be like bumping pussy's if we slept together," he said.

I was floored. I ordered more drinks to deliberately get myself drunk and we stayed out all night until the next morning. March 6th had come at the right time. I was embarrassed after spilling my guts to Jason the night before and I wanted to leave Miami. The next day I helped Jason move to the Clay Hotel, the best deal on South Beach where the television series *Miami Vice* was filmed in the eighties. We locked up our bags in the hotel's lockers so I was able to take one more run around South Beach without the bags.

"Hi can I have a Supper Shuttle take me to the airport?" I asked the dispatcher at the end of the phone.

"Where are you being picked up?" he asked.

"The Clay Hotel on Collins Avenue," I said.

"What is your name?" he asked.

"Michael," I said.

"Michael, give me fifteen minutes," he said and hung up.

In fifteen minutes the Supper Shuttle picked me up.

"Michael, we'll talk when I get back to New York," Jason said as he wrapped his arms around me.

"Bye Jason, be good," I said.

"I always am! Good-bye," he said.

The shuttle whisked me away to the airport where I caught a flight from Miami to JFK. During the flight I was nervous since I was traveling by myself. Jason stayed in Miami for a few days and was returning Thursday.

My head started to hurt and I felt pressure building up in my head. Holding my nose I blew air out, trying to relieve the pressure. My supply of gum ran out before I got to the airport and I did not stop for a new pack. Chewing gum relieved the pressure. When the plane landed, I took a cab to 125th Street and Lexington Avenue in Manhattan, and then caught the number five train to 149th Street in the Bronx. By the time I walked home it was one o'clock in the morning.

When I walked through the apartment door everyone was asleep. I headed to my room and tossed my clothing on the chair before my desk as I disrobed. Grabbing my towel from behind my door hanging on the door hook, I headed to the bathroom across the hall. I Felt sweaty from the plane ride and the long trip home from the airport. I needed a nice hot shower. My head was warm and felt like it was buzzing. I dried my hair and body then wrapped my towel around me. The steam from the shower rose above me as I exited the bathroom and headed for my bedroom.

After putting on a pair of shorts and fresh white T-shirt, I slipped into bed dreading the fact that I had to be at work at 9:00am-seven hours away. In the morning I awoke to Ma's voice.

"Theresa you'll be late for school!" she yelled.

Theresa was staying with us at the time. She instructed her to get ready for school like she did us when we were her age. Theresa was a stocky teenager with thick brown hair that caressed her shoulders and a pug nose that extended before her face. Any little gesture made her laugh.

"Hurry up or you will be late for school," Ma yelled from the dining room.

"I'm coming Grandma," she yelled back to Ma.

It sounded like Ma was rushing to get her morning routine started and Theresa was caught in the midst of the pressure. As I tried to lift my head from my pillow, once again I felt the pressure building up in my head and my mind began to play tricks on me. In my head each thought was associated with any outside stimulation that my eyes focused on. I looked across the room at my bookcase and my vision was blurry. The clothes that I left on my chair the night before resembled a person sitting. It looked as if a person was typing away at my old college typewriter.

Looking at my alarm clock I quickly jumped out of the bed and ran into the bathroom to wash up–got dressed and headed out to work. I was already thirty minutes late. When I got to work I concocted a story that my plane had arrived late and I was not able to get enough sleep. My co-worker looked at me in disbelief and told me not to worry, that my supervisor had not returned from Miami herself. As my co-worker told me this, my thoughts began to race and my mind began to create a story which I believed was true.

My supervisor at work, who was also in Miami the same time I visited, was the wife of a mobster and the FBI was monitoring my whereabouts. All I kept thinking about was that the FBI believed I was mixed up in illegal drug smuggling that was linked to dead bodies that turned up throughout New York City. The evidence that was found at the scene of the crimes proved that the deaths were mob hits and the law firm I worked for was directly involved in the foul play.

I quickly went to my desk, sat down and tried to quiet my mind. Placing my forehead on the desk and taking a deep breath I began to pray for my lunch hour to come. At noon my co-worker came to my desk.

"Hey Michael, where are you going for lunch?" she asked.

"I don't know," I said lifting my head off the desk.

"Would you like to go out with me for sushi?" she asked.

"I don't know," I said.

"Come on, you can tell me all about your trip to Miami," she insisted.

"OK just give me a minute. I have to go to the rest room. I'll meet you by the elevator," I said.

* * * *

While in the rest room I looked at myself in the mirror over the sink. Turning on the faucet I cupped my hands, leaned over and splashed cold water on my face. My face and head were warm. Drying my face off with paper towels I left the bathroom remembering that I was going to lunch with my co-worker and met her by the elevator.

"Are you OK Michael?" she asked.

"I'm just a bit tired, I told you I didn't get enough sleep last night," I explained.

"You can't have jet lag, Miami and New York are in the same time zone," she said.

"I know, it's just that I need sleep," I said.

"Here we are," she said as she held the restaurant door open for me.

After having sushi with my co-worker for lunch, I left her quickly and returned to our office building. By then I began to think secret agents were recording my every move. As the events were taking place in my head, it felt like they were really happening. Since my supervisor was not in I left work early.

By the time I arrived home my head was tingling, and it felt like my brain was working on overdrive. In my head I felt the humming of a running computer. When I walked through the door, Ma looked at me with concern.

"Are you feeling alright?" she asked.

"I'm OK," I said.

"You don't look well," she said.

I went straight to my room, then placed my backpack by my desk, took off my coat and called Jason who I had left in Miami. Jason was due home at six thirty that evening. I began rambling to him on the telephone.

"Take it easy, Michael," Jason said.

"What do you mean?" I asked.

"You just got back from vacation, you should be relaxed," he said.

"I am relaxed," I said.

"Go do something fun like plant flowers in the lawn down stairs in front of your building," he said.

Quickly my mind decided that the phone was tapped and that someone was listening to my conversation. I thought that Jason was telling me to plant drugs in the front of the building and abruptly discontinued the conversation then hung up the phone.

After that call I went into the bathroom and undressed to take a shower. Hot water poured down my back and relaxed me, quieting my mind. Drying off I went into my bedroom, tucked myself in bed and tried to sleep as my mind raced. Eventually I fell asleep and woke up the next morning feeling tired. Slowly rising out of the bed I walked to the bathroom to get ready for work. As I looked in the cabinet mirror on the wall I heard Pa in the dining room adjusting his radio.

The electromagnetic static sent chills up my spine as he locked on to the station *1010 WINS* on the AM dial. As the radio announcer read off the new headlines, my mind associated the events being announced on the radio with events that occurred in my life. My brain made connections between the people in my life and the lives of people in Washington D.C. and the Clinton administration.

They were all a part of a vast conspiracy that was being revealed to me. It explained why a certain person in Washington had committed suicide. A car alarm went off in the distance and this was a warning signal to me that a bomb was planted under Pa's car to get rid of my family because I knew. Grabbing the sides of my head with both hands, I looked into the mirror before me.

"No, don't go!" I screamed to Uriel and my niece Theresa who Uriel was about to drop off at school.

"Relax, Michael," Uriel said standing in the doorway to the bathroom as Theresa stood behind her giggling.

Standing there facing the mirror I resembled Edward Munch's *The Scream*. I thought I had to protect my family. Then the thoughts of suicide entered my mind. If I killed myself it would be all over. Ma came rushing down the hallway and was able to recognize right away, as she passed the bathroom and saw me standing before the mirror, that something was wrong with me.

"Benjamin, I need to take Michael to the hospital," she yelled to him.

She pulled me out of the bathroom and guided me across the hall to my bedroom.

"Get dressed, Michael," she said.

Ma then turned around and headed to Benjamin's room.

"Go down stairs and warm up the car," she told him.

As I slowly put on a pair of jeans and a sweatshirt, Ma entered my bedroom to get me. We left the apartment to the car, where Benjamin was waiting for us. After the thermometer of the car was one quarter between the mid point of cold and hot, Benjamin pulled out and headed for Bronx Lebanon Hospital.

Benjamin dropped Ma and I in front of the emergency entrance of the hospital then went to find a parking spot. Ma and I entered the emergency waiting room and were asked by the nurse at the front desk if I had ever been there before.

"Yes, he was at the old Bronx Lebanon," Ma said.

Yeah, I thought to myself, I was at the old Bronx Lebanon the night we had to take her to the hospital while she was in a drunken stupor wheeling a shopping cart. Feeling dizzy and weak I leaned over and fell as Benjamin came in the emergency waiting room area and caught me before I hit the floor. He and Ma helped me to a seat as the nurse returned with a medical form I was required to fill out before the doctor saw me. After some time the nurse finally brought me into the emergency room.

"Lay here on the bed till the doctor is available to see you," she said.

"Who's his doctor?" Ma asked as the nurse ignored her and walked away.

As I waited, I saw my life passing before my eyes. My mind was racing and as people passed by me, in my mind I thought they represented people I had met in the past. While my mind raced, a huge woman beside me began screaming obscenities, and had to be restrained by six staff members. On a diagonal I could see a man lying on a bed surrounded by doctors who were administering CPR, then used a defibrillator to revive him. The doctors were unsuccessful and stopped trying. As one doctor turned she saw me starring in her direction at the dead body and pulled the curtain that hung from the ceiling to shield the corpse.

There must have been a lack in the synchronism between my neurons as they passed chemical to electrical impulses between one another because my thoughts shifted to every object that moved before me and connected it to other thoughts and ideas. My brain was warm from all the work it was doing. The doctors whose job it was to help me finally came over one by one to get my story. They were unable to figure out my narrative. The doctor turned to Ma and Benjamin.

"Can you explain to me what is the matter?" asked the doctor.

"He came home from work and started acting strange," Ma said.

"He's afraid of things, he thinks people are after him," Benjamin said.

"He won't respond when we try to talk to him," Ma said.

After Ma and Benjamin explained to them what had happened to me, the doctors decided upon a battery of tests. The first test was a computerized axial tomography (CAT) scan of my head. As I waited for the CAT scan to be taken I pulled the sheet off the hospital bed and wrapped myself in it. I hopped off the bed and started walking down the hospital corridor thinking in my mind that I was the second coming, the Messiah.

God had sent me there for a purpose, but for what? Neither I, nor the doctors knew what was wrong with me. The results of the CAT scan and blood work did not reveal any abnormalities. In a last ditch effort, the doctors decided to do a spinal tap. That was one of the most painful experiences I have ever had, in addition to the beating I got the night Benjamin and I set the fire on Jackson Avenue.

It felt like my nerve was burning when the doctor inserted the needle between my vertebra twice to retrieve and replace the fluid. With all that poking and prodding they were lucky I did not get an erection like I did the day of

147

my first check up with the school doctor at P.S. 21. Even with the spinal tap, the doctors did not figure out what was wrong with me. The results of the test were normal, but my behavior was not.

"Can you explain to me what is wrong with my son?" Ma asked.

She demanded to know what was wrong with me.

"We really don't know what is wrong," the triage doctor told Ma.

They were stumped and the only thing they thought of was to refer us to Albert Einstein Hospital. When we got to Albert Einstein Hospital we were then referred to Jacobi Hospital.

"They are giving us the run around," Ma said.

"Why won't they help him," said Benjamin

"They don't know what they are doing, let's get out of here" Ma said.

At Jacobi Hospital, I was locked in a room with other people who were exhibiting similar behaviors. There I continued to experience my mind racing with a few hallucinations and delusions.

With the ability to see into the future, I envisioned myself as a homeless man eating and sleeping on a park bench. Benjamin went to a Chinese restaurant across the street from the hospital and brought me an order of chicken and broccoli with white rice. Not having eaten all day, I was starving. It was nine o'clock in the evening and after going to three hospitals one after the other, with each doctor I saw not being able to explain what was wrong with me, I was worn out.

At Jacobi, the doctors had decided like the others to refer me to yet another hospital, a psychiatric hospital on the Upper East Side of Manhattan. The head physician turned to Ma.

"Since your son has good health insurance, he will get better treatment and services at Metropolitan," he said.

"Is there nothing you can do for him here?" Ma asked.

"It would be best if he went to the psychiatric ward at Metropolitan Hospital," said the doctor.

Before I was discharged, I had to sign a bunch of documents stating that I was willingly committing myself to the psychiatric hospital. It took a long time before I finished reading the documents in front of me and knew it was in my best interest to sign.

The heat in my head was radiating and thoughts were rapidly going through my mind. As soon as I signed the papers, the orderlies placed me on a stretcher and wheeled me to an ambulette that was waiting to transport me to Metropolitan. The EMT driver was in a hurry to transport me.

"Wait till I bring my car around so that I can follow the ambulette," Benjamin told the EMT driver.

"We need to leave soon," said the EMT driver.

The ambulette flew down the FDR Drive with its sirens blaring and arrived at the hospital within forty-five minutes. At Metropolitan, I was put through yet another extensive intake and then admitted. They prescribed 20 mg of Haldol and 5 mg of Cogentin, and a nurse forced me to take the pills by threatening to administer the medication to me in needle form if I did not take it orally. It was then that I realized that I, like Kate Millet, was taking *The Loony Bin Trip*.

The last hospital stay lasted for three days. During my stay Flora, Melissa, Ruth, and Benjamin came to visit me. All the time I never wanted to be home, but after having this experience, home was not such a bad place.

Medication and meals were administered like clockwork. There were also groups for the patients to attend that helped me improve so that I could leave. By the third day, I was ready to go. The day I was released from Metropolitan, I was given an appointment with the psychiatrist who treated me for a follow up, and a referral to Pride House Psychotherapy Associates for an appointment to see a therapist who specialized in working with the "homosexual" population. The process of healing began.

A few days after my discharge from the hospital I had a moment of reconciliation with Pa. Twenty years had passed and I was feeling as if my life was not worth living. I was recovering from the breakdown and felt I had lost all reason to live–that my life lacked meaning. As I lay in bed recovering from deep depression, I heard my father rattling pots in the kitchen. I thought about him and the father-son relationship we never had, I knew something had to give. I needed my father. Even with the possibility that it was him who showed Douglas how to be a sexual predator, I still seeked his love.

Pulling myself out of bed I headed down the hallway and into the kitchen where my father stood wiping off the stove. For a split second I could feel the cotton T-shirt wiping off my back. As he stopped and turned to look at me I wrapped my arms around him.

"I love you Pa," I said.

"I love you too," he told me.

In my mind I no longer had to pretend that I was a horse and work hard for approval, or struggle for my father's love. As I hugged him I patted his back three times like I did the horses when he took me to the racetrack as a child.

"Hey watch it," he said as he pulled away from me.

"Isn't hey something horses ate?" I thought still having psychotic associations.

Feeling like he was trying to tell me something, I read into his behavior and thought he was indicating to me that three pats on the back was a sign to watch out. I quickly turned around and went back to my room.

My father does not hold against me what happened at such a young age but it did affect our relationship. I can look at old photos of the two of us and know that we were once very close. Today there is still little communication between us, but it has been made clear that we love each other. It took an acute psychiatric breakdown to overcome the fear I developed to let my father know I always loved him.

It was done, I had finally let Pa know that I loved him regardless of what I thought I knew and regardless of what was happening to me. Inside I felt satisfied that if anything did happen to me, he knew how I felt about him. It is a slow process but little by little my father and I are communicating and developing the father-son relationship that was lost. In the beginning, the healing process was difficult. When I met with the psychiatrist on the follow up visit we discussed my progress and the medications.

"The side effects of the medications are unbearable," I said.

"What side effects are you experiencing?" he asked.

"Dry mouth, my joints are tight, my face is starting to twitch, nausea, dizziness," I said.

"I understand," he said looking at me with concern.

Together we experimented with an array of drugs. He prescribed them and I took them. Feeling like a guinea pig I tried Haldol, Zyprexa, and Risperidone to relieve the psychotic symptoms I was experiencing. Cogentin, which was prescribed to limit the side effects of the medication, really did not take the side effects away. The psychiatrist also prescribed Paxil, Zoloft, and Lithium, to help with the depression. The mood stabilizer Depakote was also prescribed but that is where I drew the line. Depakote was not an option, as I had heard of a person on Depakote committing suicide.

Overcoming my struggle reinforced my desire to live. This desire to live was nurtured by returning to work and continuing to take academic classes at Hunter College. Life was not easy for me, and as I pressed to get better, I relapsed because of not following the instructions of the medications I was prescribed.

The dosages my psychiatrist prescribed were too strong. Taking it upon myself to adjust the dosages, I cut the pills in half or took less of them till I felt like my old self, without the depression and psychotic symptoms. That was my Diagnostic and Statistical Manual (DSM) diagnosis' Major Depression with Psychotic features. My experience was not a single episode, since I relapsed every time I was put under stress.

When the workload at my job increased or I was preparing for an upcoming exam at school, I developed psychotic symptoms and relapsed, spending most of my time at home in bed resting. My relapses led me to a cycle of enlightenment and darkness. While at home I got a vision of a bright light that illuminated my mind, an experience that is usually described by those who have had a brush with death and think that they are in the presence of God. During my periods of illumination, I believed God was sending me the key to the universe, the cosmic code, and I jotted fragments of the code down as my mind was racing to understand it all.

Believing that I was the chosen one to get the one verse that named God's soul, I tried to decipher the code. In the code it was revealed to me that my life was part of God's design, just like the day I sat on the park bench behind Bronxville intending to end my life, in a whisper God's universe was explained to me. The lives on earth are a part of God's soul in motion-movement from one body to the next, passing in the electromagnetic currents not visible to the eye.

Chapter X:
An Angel Gets its Wings

Although I was still in the process of healing, it was time for me to get out and begin living again. Having spent so much time in bed I was once again ready to create a new life for myself. I went out as soon as I was physically able. It was gay pride month and I wanted to be at the Gay Pride parade. Flora was on her way over to visit Ma and pick me up. She wanted to help get me out of the house and start living again.

We headed down to Christopher Street in Greenwich Village to watch the festivities and the boys. In the afternoon we ended up at the pier. This was something I usually did with Jason and tried to call him before Flora and I left but he did not answer the phone. While we were on the pier, Flora hooked up with a couple of lesbians who probably thought she was gay. Angela was among them.

Angela was physically beautiful, a mixture of Spanish and French decent. Flora and I became very good friends with Angela. Angela was attracted to Flora and did what she could to become close to her. Later on we found out that Angela also took Depakote.

"You take it too?" Angela asked with a sense of happiness that she was not alone.

"Yeah, but I don't take it, my doctor prescribes too much," I said.

"I take 500 mg twice a day," she said.

As we swapped med stories she always talked about how she had more psychotic symptoms when taking the medication than when not taking it. Once during a relapse and in a psychotic state, I believed God had put Angela in my life to marry and have children. As Flora hung out with Angela and her new friends that day on the pier, I sat up against a fence near the water and was approached by a young man.

"I'm interested in getting to know you, you good looking guy," he said.

"Thank you," I replied.

It was nice that other guys were interested in me. I also thought I looked good with all the weight I lost during my period of depression.

"My name is Joseph," he said.

"I'm Michael, nice to meet you," I said.

We exchanged numbers and hooked up a few times after that day. Together we traveled to Excalibur, a gay club in New Jersey, and danced the night away. Flora and Angela met us there on occasion. We had a blast. Angela acted the fool to make my sister laugh in hopes of bringing them closer and winning her love.

I was able to see right through Angela's intentions. Joseph exhibited similar behavior with me. Deep down he was a good-hearted guy but was moving too fast for me.

"Come out with me to New Jersey?" he asked.

"I'll think about it," I said.

He showed me around, bought me gifts and constantly talked to me about moving in with him. The thought of living with another man and making another commitment really frightened me. Having someone interested in me made me think of my past relationship with Patrick.

Patrick was out of my life for a while but I still had the memories of our relationship and I found myself occasionally trying to push the thoughts of us together out of my head. I think I was suffering from Post-Traumatic Stress Disorder not only from my distant past but also from the traumatic separation that I had experienced with Patrick. Little by little I fazed Joseph out of my life and retreated to spending time with Jason and Angela, hanging out and going club hopping, trying to enjoy myself.

Having a good time was not that difficult because the medication I was taking was affecting my mood. Early in the day I was taking the antidepressant Paxil to lift my depression and boy did it work. Twenty minutes after taking the pill I felt like I was invincible. I would be walking down the street with Jason and burst into song. It also made me feel energized, like I wanted to have sex, but at the same time it prevented me from getting an erection.

In the evening it was a different story, I took the anti-psychotic Haldol and my mood became somber. My thoughts were also quieted. The pills also made me tire easily. My desire to dance was lessened and I did not have the energy to stay out all night until five the next morning like I use to do with Jason.

On many of the nights I went out with Jason I hooked up with guys, having one-night stands and dating, until I learned as much about their sexual behavior as possible. I was not looking for a match, I was trying to collect data on guys who were out looking for a sexual hook-up to find out their motivations and learn more about the behavior of people on the prowl for sex. A part of me was also searching for someone to fill the void in my life and it ended when I realized I had to fill the void with me and not run away from myself and what happened to me as a child.

When I finally accepted who I was and what had happened to me, it was November 12, 1995. This was the date I met Lyle. Jason and I got together that evening to go out dancing. I explained to Jason before we went in to Champs, a sports bar in Chelsea, that I was ready to have someone in my life again. It was less than a year from the time I broke up with Patrick.

After my breakup with Patrick, I spent a lot of time in bed thinking and getting to know myself and what was right for me. That night was going to be the time when I met the right person. Ready to give life and relationships another chance I headed for the center of the dance floor when we entered the bar. The music was pulsing and there Lyle appeared before me across the dance floor.

From the moment I laid eyes on him, I knew he was my soul mate. As I danced in one spot on the dance floor, my eyes gazed over in his direction in hopes of drawing him near me. Jason tired easily that night. No sooner had we arrived at the club he felt like he wanted to leave. After a couple of songs he headed home. Jason usually stayed dancing around me all night like a bodyguard giving guys dirty looks of disapproval to keep them away from me. There was something different about this night. Jason seemed to be letting go.

Ever since the time we met and I told him of my attraction and love for him during our trip to Miami, he seemed to protect me, just as I protected that little sparrow I caught in my youth. Jason knew I had the desire to live and love. That night he seemed to let me go and I took the opportunity to try and spread my wings but I was unable to; it was like I had no wings to fly. Looking back, I should have let that sparrow go. Trying to hold on to the love that it gave me resulted in its death. After that night Jason was no longer acting as my bodyguard and shielding me.

Now that Jason was gone, Lyle drew nearer until we were dancing in front of one another. The DJ changed songs and I took the opportunity to initiate a conversation.

"I'm taking a rest, want to join me?" I asked.

"Sure," he said.

We walked off the dance floor and sat on bar stools up against the wall directly in front of the dance floor and watched the dancers.

"I like that green hat your wearing," he said as his arm extended upwards towards my head.

"Don't touch the hat," I said when he went to reach for it.

"Let's go for a coffee," I told him trying not to appear too defensive and indicating to him that I was interested.

"Have you ever been to the Big Cup?" I asked.

"No," he said.

"It's a coffee house a few blocks away," I said.

"Good, we can talk without having to shout over the loud music," he said.

At the Big Cup Lyle and I ordered a coffee and a piece of German Chocolate cake to share. Sharing a meal is sacred for some people and I think this gesture brought the two of us closer that night.

"What are your intentions?" I asked.

"I just want to have a good time," he said.

After a long talk we left the cafe.

"Would you like a ride to the train station?" he asked.

"Sure, I need to get the Lexington Avenue line," I said.

As he drove me to the nearest train station to get back home to the Bronx I thought about his response in the coffee house and figured I will really give him a good time tonight.

"Don't you want to have sex? " I asked.

"OK," he said with enthusiasm.

We went to his apartment that night. Having sex the first night was not a typical one-night stand. Feeling a connection on an emotional level that first night I was with him made it feel special. When I met him, he had a genuine quality that he still has to this day. He is the type of guy in the sense that what you see is what you get, what you get is good and what I know deep down inside every gay man wants.

The next morning Lyle called in sick to work and we spent some of the day together. I had stopped working at the time and was still a student at Hunter. Lyle pulled out a Cat Stevens album and played *Father and Son*-how did he know that was my favorite song? Things just felt right with him. It was strange since I only knew him for a few hours but I felt like we were meant to be together. Lyle and I had breakfast and exchanged our telephone numbers.

A week later I was back at Champs, I had such a good time the last time I was there that I decided to go back.

"Jason I had a really nice night last Thursday with a guy I met named Lyle," I said.

"Who's Lyle?" he asked.

"I met him at Champs the other night after you left," I said.

"Is he cute?" he asked.

"Yeah," I said.

"Is he hung?" he asked.

That was typical of Jason, looks and packaging was all that was most important. Everything else didn't really matter.

"Do you want to go back to Champs with me tonight, yes or no?" I asked.

"Yeah, we'll go around 7:30," he said

While at Champs that night we ran into Lyle. I was surprised to see him there. Jason and I approached him and I introduced Jason to him. Inside it felt like my neurons were firing and I felt nervous. He didn't seem too thrilled to see me but I was determined to be with him. In time Lyle's attitude seemed to change, and my life rapidly took a turn for the better. Feeling like I wanted to be with Lyle, I no longer felt like meeting guys on the prowl.

After 10 months Lyle and I were an item traveling together. I sat in the passengers seat as we headed west on Interstate-90 from Massachusetts to New York at 70 miles per hour. We had out run a hurricane that made its way to the shore of Provincetown. Just an hour and a half ago I was standing across the street from the *Sun Set Inn*, a lovely bed and breakfast. Lyle was on the phone checking in with his cousin to find out the condition of his grandfather.

"How is he?...What did the nurse say?...I'll be there soon," Lyle said as he hung up the phone. From his facial expression, I could tell the report was not a good one. After the call we both quickly crossed the street and headed up to our room to gather the belongings we just unpacked. When we packed up all our belongings we knocked next door to Ian's room to let him know that we had to leave. It was obvious by the expression on Ian's face that he was not too happy about our quick departure. It was Lyle's ex-boyfriend Ian who gave Lyle and I the idea to visit Cape Cod that week.

"You have to go to Provincetown, it's a must," Ian had said.

"What's so good about it?" Lyle asked.

"It's so gay!" Ian said.

Ian spoke of Provincetown so highly and being new in the relationship with Lyle I thought it would be nice to get away somewhere gay friendly, a place where we felt comfortable walking down the street hand in hand. Walking hand in hand is something two gay men can do in Greenwich Village and not feel self-conscious. Ian gave me the impression that love between two gay men can be easily exhibited in Provincetown without the fear of gay bashing, so we accepted the idea of going there for a vacation.

Standing in the lobby we explained to Ian why we had to stop our vacation before we started it and apologized for canceling our reservation–we headed to the old Subaru he named Madam Blavadsky with the hole in the floor where my feet rest on the passengers side and pulled out of the parking lot. We did not even have time to go to the beach, the main reason we went there in the first place. Driving west on Route 6 we did however did get a glimpse of the dunes as we passed through each town on the Cape.

Lyle quickly cut through traffic on Route 6 to I-495 then on to I-90, leaving behind the large clusters of dark storm clouds and gusty winds. Heading in the direction of his childhood home I tried to keep myself occupied by taking out an old note pad and began writing the first few lines of the new novel I was planning to write. Our relationship was a few months old, so the details of his roots were not fully disclosed. Beginning with his name was a good place to start I thought and was quite surprised when I learned that Lyle literally means "of the Island."

Could it be? I asked myself. Yes, *Of the Island* will be the name of the best selling great gay novel. It sounded like a good idea that needs some care and feeding. That is exactly what Nobert Weiner might have thought and I hopefully believed was the beginning. My idea to start writing a love story between two gay men that would be a best seller just came to mind and I jotted down a few lines as Lyle drove. That's it, a story about two gay men who met one another at a bar and lived happily ever after, I thought to myself.

The phrase "happily ever after" is a fiction, because life has more than its ups. Life definitely has its downs, and this time in Lyle's and my own life, it was definitely a down time. I became depressed realizing that we were still courting, so I did not have much to go on for inspiration to write the great gay novel. Having been in a relationship with Patrick for three and a half years would provide some material but a true love story ends when both lives leave the earth still as one, just as in the film *Thelma and Louise.*

After considering my past and current situation, I knew all the details were going to have to come from my creative imagination. As my mind wondered, we reached exit 7 on I-90 and headed south through Rennsselear to the Amtrak Station. During the ride there was much silence. I know Lyle was preoccupied trying to keep an eye on the road and contemplating the worst of his grandfather's situation. Good-byes were said as soon as Lyle pulled into the parking lot of the station.

"I love you Lyle," I softly said through the window of the car.

"I love you too," he responded in a flat tone.

As I watched him drive away, I could see by the furrowing of his brow through the windshield, turning the wheel of Madam Blavatsky, and the speed with which he drove off, that he knew his grandfather was near death. At that moment it was difficult trying not to think of the old wives' tale that death comes in three's. Ironically, this was the third time in my life I was in the Albany area.

The first time I performed at the Empire State Plaza when I was in High School. I remember dancing, an African dance that symbolized the transformation of young pubescent African boys from childhood to adulthood. The torch and traditions were transferred from the elder male tribe members before dying off to the younger boy members, symbolizing the passing of time. There wasn't much that I learned from my father when I reached puberty, and I know Lyle didn't learned much from his father as a child.

Lyle was raised by his grandparents, French Canadians who migrated from Quebec at the turn of the 20th Century. Not having our biological father available as we grew was something Lyle and I had in common.

Lyle was already four years old when my grandmother passed and Ma stood in the kitchen banging her head up against the wall while she was pregnant with me, and his own father had remarried after his biological mother passed away a year before of a brain aneurysm. Unlike my parents who met during a period where the need to survive was the motivation to unite, his parents met at Guptill's Skating Rink in upstate Cohoes during a night of fun in the late 1950's. His father remarried soon after his mother's death, it appears in an attempt to fill a void that was once filled with beauty.

His mother was a beautiful woman who resembled the classic fifties debutante with porcelain skin. Her beauty is seen in Lyle. He is of average height with light brown hair and eyes that change color with the seasons. Like the smile on his mother's face in old photographs, Lyle brightens up the grayest of days. It was the darkest day in Lyle's father's life when his mother passed, but he had to move on to try to regain the feeling only true love can bring and she was the only true love in his life that was now and forever gone.

Unfortunately, the void continued in a father-son relationship that was far off and distant. Looking at Lyle, it only makes sense that his father kept his distance; the reminder of lost love was too strong. It was obvious that whenever he gazed upon his son he only saw the beauty of his lost wife. His mother's soft hands nurtured Lyle's first 18 months of life. Her softness is a characteristic reflected in Lyle's personality. 18 months after his birth the beauty in both their lives was gone.

The train was about to leave the station, so I quickly purchased a one-way ticket to New York City and boarded the 1:35 southbound train to Penn Station. My desire to get home made it feel like time was at a stand still. Not knowing what to expect as I was getting to my destination, I hoped that everything was going to be all right for Lyle. As I entered the train I noticed it was quite crowded that afternoon.

It appeared as if many tourists were leaving from Montreal to New York. Feeling tense and thinking about Lyle and how he must be feeling, I just wanted to sit in quiet and try reading to occupy my mind. My bookmark indicated to me that I was half way through to finishing Thomas Hardy's *Jude the Obscure.* As I walked through the first train car I heard idle chatter in French.

"Combien de temps?" a man asked his companion as I passed.

"Sit still," a woman was telling a young child beside her.

165

Continuing to proceed through the dining car, I finally settled in the next car beside the window. Making myself comfortable one row past the bathroom, thinking I would have easy access if I needed to go, I opened my book and began to read. As I read about Jude, he was living with Sue in Aldbrickham continuing their relations as they did when they were in Shaston, and I began to reflect back on the drive to the station and my idea to write the novel.

I closed the book and took a few seconds to review my notes, I then put them away and went back to reading Hardy, realizing that Jude himself was not having such a good time with life. He was physically and emotionally ill. Being reminded of how I truly felt at the time I looked at my watch and realized that I was only an hour and a half into my trip and how much I missed Lyle already. This was one relationship I knew was meant to be. Yeah, many people say it was love at first sight when they meet their partners, but this was one union that makes such a cliché ring true.

I went back to reading and finished another chapter of Hardy when the train pulled into Penn Station. Thirsty and feeling dehydrated I was out of luck since the food car had already closed. After departing the train I headed to catch the number two train to the Bronx and stopped into the Nathan's in Penn Station to grab a soft drink. Before I finished my bottle of Poland Spring water, I was in the Bronx explaining to my family what my brief stay in Provincetown was like and why I was home from vacation so soon.

Uriel was in the dining room with Ma as I explained to them what the dunes in Hyannis look like. Reminding them that this was my second trip to Provincetown I described the old buildings, what town life is like and all of the fun things to do there, like whale watching. They both looked a bit confused as I tried to describe the place.

"It is an old fishing town. It is at the tip of Cape Cod in Massachusetts. The only difference between that village and City Island in the Bronx is that it has a large gay population. As you walk through the town there are rainbow flags everywhere symbolizing gay pride. There are cafes where men sit having coffee dressed in drag, just hanging out. It is like Greenwich Village here in New York, but it's in a fishing village," I said.

For a moment I felt like Ian explaining Provincetown to Lyle and me, he seemed to convince both of us to go there the first time. Uriel and Ma looked at me with disbelief as both their heads turned from the television. The thunder and rushing waves of the Gordon's Fisherman commercial got their attention.

"Trust the Gordon's Fisherman," the television blared.

That was exactly the type of message I was trying to convey: trust me, believe what I am telling you, but with a gay flair. Because of the poor stereotypical jokes about female lesbians, the association with fish quickly made me think of the female sex and quickly exclaim:

"There are a lot of lesbian couples there too," thinking they'd understand what I was trying to share with them.

Ever since I can remember being comfortable with my sexuality and loving myself as a gay man, I wanted my family to share the joy that I experience as a gay man. The phone rang and Uriel quickly got up to answer it.

"Hello,...Oh Hi Flora,...You want to speak to Ma?... Here Ma its Flora," she said as she handed the phone over to Ma.

Flora is the only one in my family who I believe truly knows what a gay experience is like. She never to my knowledge had a gay sexual experience but she has attended the gay pride parade in New York and talks to me about my relationships with men, like she talks about her relationships with men to her friends.

When Flora and I met Angela at gay pride they quickly hit it off. They hit it off so well that Angela started to develop feelings for Flora that Flora could not handle. When Flora and I spoke of our relationships it was always clear that Flora was heterosexual. She did develop a friendly love for Angela, a love of unconditional acceptance like one family member has for another.

It almost appeared incestuous-the closeness they shared-like Gena Davis and Susan Sarandon in *Thelma and Louise*. Sadly Angela went off her roof alone in a successful suicide attempt during what I am sure was a full-blown psychotic state. Angela was physically beautiful with a ruff edge that Flora smoothed the longer they hung out together. Her death motivated me to live life to its fullest and enjoy those around me.

"Hold on Flora, someone is on the other line...Hello... Oh Hi Lyle...Yeah he's here...Just a second I'm on the other line...Flora, Lyle is on the other line for your brother...I'll talk to you later...OK?.. Love you too...bye...Here you go... it's Lyle," Ma said as she handed me the phone. No sooner did I get home did Lyle call.

"Hi, Michael?" he asked.

"Hi Lyle, it's me Michael."

He began talking to me with his voice low and softer than usual. I had the feeling in my gut that something was very wrong.

"How's your grandfather?" I asked.

"He passed away a little while after I got here," he said.

"Did you get to talk to him," I asked.

"Yes, I think he was waiting for me to come home," he said.

"Do you mean he died just after you got home?" I asked.

"Yes," he said.

"I'm sorry," I said.

I could feel the corner of my lips drop, not knowing what to say; those two words came out of my mouth. Trying to focus on the positive I forced myself to think with death comes life. Life was at a down point but soon to rise. That day I did not make it to Green Island, but I was curious to learn about the secrets that small island held.

Lyle was not aware of the secret life I was living before we met. Before meeting Lyle, my life had changed one weekend as Jason and I walked around Chelsea.

"Wait for me here, I have to use the bathroom" I told Jason.

"Don't take too long," he said.

As Jason stood outside Rome, a gay bar, I entered and went to the bathroom. While inside, I descended a staircase to the rest rooms. An older man was waiting outside the men's room and grabbed his crotch as I passed him indicating that he wanted to fool around, so I grabbed his shirt and dragged him into a stall and brought him and myself to pleasure.

It took a while to ejaculate because of the newly prescribed Zoloft. After I was done with him I left the bar and headed north on Ninth Avenue up to Hell's Kitchen to Jason's apartment. Since that day I felt very predatorial and began to search out sexual experiences in a way that was different from a usual night out with Jason. The predator in me had finally evolved.

* * * *

A week after Lyle's grandfather's death I was on to reading Honor de Balzac's *Pere Goriot*. Strangely enough life seemed to be mimicking literature, first with *Jude the Obscure* now with Balzac or was it vice-a-versa. Old Goriot was on his deathbed and his daughter was to inherit a fortune her sister had already spent. In Lyle's case it was a question of who was to inherit the burden of property, a modest old home with years of history on Green Island.

Ian was a real estate appraiser who was no longer romantically involved with Lyle. He was Lyle's first love, a love that today lingers in friendship. If Ian was not such a playboy and had not moved on to another relationship, that night at Champs I never would have met Lyle, nor would we have been in Provincetown the day of his grandfather's passing. As I danced facing the entrance of the club looking in Lyle's direction the night we met, there was an African American guy who crossed between Lyle and I.

Lyle glanced back at me as the African American guy passed by, and headed in my direction. It might have been someone else in my life today if Lyle was with Ian. People usually do not realize what they have until it's gone. Ian learned this lesson and he is reminded of true love every time he sees Lyle and I together.

I was jealous of Ian when I learned that Lyle had taken him to Green Island one summer and had given him the honor of meeting Mim. Ian was also introduced to Lyle's close cousin and aunt in the Village of Lake George, who owned an antique shop and who he loved very much.

One whole summer Lyle took Ian back and forth from New York to Lake George to retrieve items for their own antique business they were trying to start in the city. They set up a table at a local flea market in Chelsea and earned a small profit with Lyle having hopes of one day having his own antique shop like his aunt who help raise him. Together they traveled to Lake George for merchandise and the opportunity to share their experiences in the business with his aunt who loved him.

Ian never learned what true love is. He sure did not get it from his cold working middle class Jewish parents from Long Island who did not have time for their child as he grew. Lyle got his love from his mother's touch those first 18 months of his life and from Mim. Mim was very possessive with Lyle, keeping a close watch on him up until the day he moved to New York City to attend New York University. Her possessiveness was so strong that Lyle often felt smothered by her over protectiveness. She had to know everywhere he was and everything he was doing, not approving of his explorations.

Mim was heartbroken the day he decided to apply to colleges in New York City and really felt the loss the day he received his acceptance letter. She already had enough time raising him the right way and showing him what true love really is.

Although Ma was a welfare mother who worked around the house and told us she loved us so much that it sounded mechanical, it felt warm when she hugged us, looked into our eyes and gave us the impression that she was there if we needed her. Ian on the other hand never got that mother's touch and was molded in a roughness that requires redemption. He showed his true colors the second night I met Lyle at Champs. One could easily see that there was never any true love between them, and if there were they still would be together today.

That night the music was louder than usual. Everyone in the club was jumping and rubbing their sweaty bodies against one another as they tried to dance on the small dance floor. Madonna's *Let's get Unconscious* was playing as I saw a slightly older looking stocky built bald guy get closer to Lyle and I. He was about five feet six inches tall with piercing blue eyes, dirty blond hair and looked in Lyle's direction trying to get his attention. The stranger grew more handsome as he got closer to us. Lyle looked over at him and smiled. Live In Joy's *I'm a Dreamer* began playing and while everyone went crazy dancing around Lyle stopped moving, touched my arm and motioned toward the stocky bald guy.

"Michael this is Ian, Ian this is Michael," he said.

"Nice to meet you" I said to Ian, being kind to him not knowing the history between the two of them.

"Same here," he replied with a smug look on his face.

His tone of voice was loud trying hard to be heard over the pulsing music, revealing a cunning personality and instantly exhibiting a blunt ingenuity-he was the type of guy who wanted to live a good life at someone else's expense and that is just what he did while they were together. They met shortly after Lyle graduated from NYU.

They met at the Monster, a gay club in the Village, and from that night on till the day of their separation they were an item. During the day Ian worked as a travel agent and then a waiter while Lyle worked in the Managing Clerk's office at a Manhattan Law firm. Lyle's income paid half the bills and there was more than enough extra to live a comfortable life. Ian had to have name brands that indicated his attitude, only the best to survive including cocaine and marijuana to make reality appear better than what it was. Lyle was miserable living with Ian's need to keep up with the Jones's.

That became obvious the first time we all got together for brunch one Sunday morning. Thinking it was a nice idea to get people together in our lives since we started to date, both Lyle and I invited our close companions to meet for brunch. He invited Ian and I invited Patrick and Jason to the Garage in the West Village. Patrick was having a dispute with his current lover and was unable to make it.

"What are you having?" I asked Lyle.

"Vegetable omelet," he said.

"And you?" I asked Jason.

"Eggs Benedict," he said.

"I'm going to have a cheese omelet," said Ian.

"I think I'll have the strawberry pancakes," I told the waiter as he took our order. The brunch seem to be going well. Every one got along fine until it was time to pay the bill. After the waiter dropped the check off at our table, Ian checked out to the bathroom, not returning. We decided to pay the bill and wait for him outside the restaurant and the venom flowed.

"Did he fall in?" Jason asked.

"I'm sure he's just having a little difficulty. It's the cheese, it makes some people constipated," I said.

"Be nice," Jason said.

"Finally," Lyle said when Ian returned from the bathroom.

"Ready to go?" I asked.

"We paid the bill," Lyle said.

"We thought you died in there," said Jason as we left the restaurant.

* * * *

Up until the last days on his deathbed, Pip was in a dispute with Lyle's uncle John over who was to be the executor of his estate. As the weeks passed and Pip's condition deteriorated from cancer John tried to persuade him to change his will to make him executor. On the day of his death the decision was made, Lyle was Pip's executor and it remained that way to his death.

About the same time of Pip's passing my Aunt Roxana had control of my Aunt Rochelle's estate when she died a couple of days later. The old wives' tale was ringing true and the death of my aunt confirmed it. She was the second to go in such a short period of time. Death does come in threes. Aunt Roxana had to hire a lawyer to execute the will, unlike Lyle who handled his grandfather's affairs on his own with all the training he learned while working for lawyers.

Being a calendar clerk for a law firm at the time, I assisted Lyle by notarizing all the documents and went with him to the county clerk's office in Albany to file them. The process was becoming more and more familiar to me. Never having to deal with the issue of death before, I was now becoming acquainted with probate proceedings. Although these proceedings were new to me, legal proceedings in general were becoming a bore to me; I wanted something new and challenging to do after my psychotic break. My mind wiped the past away; it was like de-fragmenting a hard drive and putting the old files away in storage.

Now in the beginning stages of a relapse, my mind raced and I began putting bits of information together. John wanted to inherit the estate so he got an idea while he administered morphine to ease his father's pain. He intentionally increased the amount of morphine with the intent to make his father drowsy, so he would agree to a new version of his will that John took it upon himself to draw up. John intentions went awry when Pip died of an overdose, but deep down he wanted his death because he did not change the conditions of his will–keeping Lyle in charge of the estate.

Knowing that the medical examiner would deem his death a murder, he placed his body in a sage green 1970's meat freezer where the family usually kept a wealth of game they caught during deer hunting season. The body was sawed in pieces while frozen with Pips own electric buzz saw he kept on the workbench in the basement and buried the body in the crawlspace in the far back end of the basement of the old house in Green Island. John thought to do this after watching a news report on the John Wayne Gacey execution. He was lead to kill his own father just because he was not appointed executor of his father's estate. Of course, none of this was true.

"Did you take your medicine yet?" Ma yelled to me from her bedroom. I stopped working on my novel and put my pad of notes and pen on my lap.

"No Ma, I'm taking it right now," I said. Ma was always ready to administer my medication when needed.

"Don't stay up too late, you have school in the morning," she said.

"I know," I said.

"You have to give your mind some rest," she said.

"I know Ma, good night," I said.

" I'll see you in the morning if the Lord is willing," were her last words as every night since her conversion.

It was way past 11:30 p.m. and I did feel myself going off the deep end but when in the midst of the beginning of a manic phase, taking my medicatioins is the last thing on my mind. My neurons begin to fire rapidly and connect the bits and pieces of information that have been stored in my brain. The left side of my brain is on full throttle and I feel the most creative and in a hyper-aroused state. My head begins to hum like the workings of a computer hard drive. When I hear the humming sound it is like music and the urge to write comes upon me. When Ma called I was working on the first draft of my book.

The idea to write the novel just came to me, though there is more to it then just writing down ideas and thoughts, after reading Umberto Eco's *The Role of the Reader*, the writing process became more of an art. Will the novel be an open or a closed one? Eco used these terms to describe the writer's intentions and the layers of meaning that can be intertwined in a book. Layers of meaning are usually concealed in an open book. It is a closed book that one is to take at face value. What you see is what you get, or is it?

Not like Lyle, Ian was pretty much a closed book on the surface he presented as a healthy and stable gay man. When the initial veil is lifted one can see a tortured soul struggling with a past life of family neglect and another hard crust to be broken into. To get closer to who he truly was one had to break through the next layer to find a frightened individual trying to understand what true love is really about and not thinking that he'll get it since dealing with the constant thoughts of rejection from the moment he contracted the HIV virus.

Ian was not positive when Lyle brought him to upstate New York or during the time they were together. The virus was something he contracted from his new partner he left Lyle for. Coming to terms with the virus and knowing that with the new HIV cocktails contracting the virus is no longer a death sentence, Ian moved forward with life and on to other men after his lover died after a few years they were together. Ian was now casually dating the assistant he hired for his appraisal firm and others he met in the night dance club circuit.

"I saw Lyle's ex-boyfriend last night at the Limelight," Jason told me as we had a coffee at The Big Cup.

"What's his name?" he asked

"Ian," I said.

"Did you see Lyle?" I asked.

"No," he said.

My jealousy was getting the best of me and I was beginning to get possessive, but quickly put my feelings in check knowing how Lyle feels about possessive people. He was not my property, so why was I so concerned with the idea of him going out for a night on the town? It was Thursday night and Lyle had to be to work at the law firm. He was fired from a law firm a few years before I met him for coming in late, not going into work and not doing any work. It was the alcohol getting the best of him.

"Did you have fun last night?" I asked Jason.

"I was naughty," he said.

"OK...who did you take home?" I asked.

"Do you think I remember names? Just kidding... Victor," he said.

"Whose Victor?" I asked knowing Jason was going to tell me all about him and how fantastic the sex was between them.

Every time I heard this story from Jason, it was the same; the only difference was the name of the person he met. Occasionally penis size and the expression on Jason's face varied depending on how ethnic the newly met stranger was. He also redirected the conversation back to Ian. It was obvious that Jason had a crush on Ian. Ian had an alpha male-bad boy persona that even I have to admit I was attracted to.

Being sexually attracted to others was not difficult for me with my history. All those years being preyed on by my

177

brother had an impact on my psyche. By understanding his methodology and techniques, I too had the database of a sexual predator stored in me. For a second time in my life this database was being processed by my limbic system as acceptable behavior. First it was Colin, now my seat of morality was once again not responding.

The psychotropic medications I was taking had the affect of bringing certain behaviors to the surface. My mind and body wanted to use those techniques and methods to act, so that I had the feeling of control over some part of my life. What allowed me to perpetuate the act in the past successfully was the fact that my victim was an innocent and helpless child. Now it was different, when these new predatory feelings arose I was not looking for control but to understand it all. I was trying to find the answers to my life, specifically, why the sexual abuse happened to me and how to control my predatory behavior.

I knew how my brother Douglas functioned, but his was just a micro example. I needed to learn from a larger population if the methodology and techniques were the same in others because I found them in me. I believed if I understood the mind of a sexual predator, I one day would be successful in helping to stop the cycle of abuse that I am capable of perpetuating. After my successful encounter with that older man in the basement of Rome, I began to search out my prey in the hope of learning something.

Still in the process of healing from my past I felt the only way to heal was to satisfy my desire to know. I had to learn about sexual predators and what I was fighting not to become. The struggle within me and the persistent desire to know, had stayed with me since the time I entered my father's room trying to understand what was between my father's legs. The education system taught me to be a data gatherer to help feed a larger body of knowledge, and that is what I indtended to do.

The struggle within me was being resolved as I attended therapy, took the psychotropic meds and prayed hard each night before laying my head down to rest. This wasn't enough, I had to do genealogical therapy with my life to know who I was and search out predators to learn about what I thought I was becoming. The first step was purchasing a computer. I rationalized my purchase to my family and Lyle by explaining to them that I was buying it to do my schoolwork and write my novel, so as not to give my true intentions away.

The computer did help me with my homework but I knew from Jason and my earlier life experiences how the computer had other uses. Predators were getting high tech with the change in technology. The use of computers was a new way to prey on people. I thought that after connecting with a stranger online I'd exchange pics and meet them in a public place or their apartment. Before I went, I had to let Jason know where I was going and give him a copy of the person's pic I was going to meet, just in case I vanished.

I logged on to my computer and searched out those who were also on the hunt. Not wasting any time, I surfed through chat rooms with sexual themes. After surfing the net I realized that I easily cut to the chase by utilizing the member directory and searching it by using the key word sex, narrowing my search to the profile of the type of person I was looking for. After finding a profile match, I then viewed the directory to see if there was an indication telling me the person was online. If online, the "find" button was clicked to direct me to the chat room the person was located in.

Prior to entering the chat room, I read their online member profile. If the person was someone whose information passed my psycho-linguistic test, their dialogue was monitored in the chat room to confirm my earlier findings. If a person passed the second screening, they were then sent an instant message (IM) outside the chat room for a one-on-one conversation. Some times a good candidate was not in a chat room but surfing the net. In this case an intriguing IM was sent, initiating a conversation to hook their interest. Once connecting with the person a pic was exchanged to finalize the match.

During dialogue it became obvious if the person I sought out was not safe. Most of the time the person I hooked up with engaged in a safe, mutual exchange. In all the encounters I had, it was obvious that all the men I met fell into four different categories. There was type, A, B, C, and D. The first category being the A or (Act)-type, since they were focused on and interested only in the sexual act. They just wanted to satisfy their biological urge and their mind was focused on the sexual encounter. This was the category that my brother Douglas fell into. The predatory act was engaged in only to satisfy his biological urges.

When I met the A -type on line, I followed the directions given to me to a house or apartment. Once I stepped though the threshold the sexual act immediately began and as soon as the sexual act was over, good-byes were exchanged and I was escorted to the door without an invitation to stay or ever see or hear from him again. All dialogue took place prior to the encounter with little talking during the contact. Many I chatted with were men and women who were eager to have cyber sex and no additional contact. The guy who approached me as a teen while I was playing hooky from

JHS 161 and had his way with me in the old abandoned school building was a Type-A predator also.

The B or (Boyish)-type predator was the second type I encountered. These were men who were only fixated on young boys. They were looking to hook up with children. Presenting to them as if I were young, with the use of the psycho-linguistic level of a child, this type of predator was rein in. I was not interested to hook up with this type of individual but entertained myself to learn from their methods.

This B-type had a way of setting the stage in their dialogue to help gain the trust of their future victim. There was a system to their approach and interaction with me that hit close to home. These types of interactions reminded me of the way my brother Douglas got me to partake in his sexual games. This type does not discriminate by sex. There were also men I encountered who mistook me for a young girl and pursued me until I mentioned I was male.

The third type of sexual predator I encountered I call the C or (Companionship)-type because they were most concerned with companionship. With this type, there was more to it than the sexual encounter. These types of predators were looking for companionship rather than sex. The idea of the sexual act may have helped drive their behavior to act out sexually, but there was more behind it.

These encounters involved people who were looking for companionship or someone else to connect with in a non-sexual way. They were lonely and dealing with other life situations and they needed to be with someone else for a brief moment in time to help forget it. Although looking for a release from their life problems, they sexualized their feelings and engaged in sex for a release. There was much more dialogue before, during and after the sexual encounter. I seemed to feel like I belonged to this group.

The majority of the C-type predators I encountered were more open about themselves and tried to stay in touch with me, giving me information so that I'd contact them in the future if I so wished to do so. This was not my intention. I was looking for and trying to compile data. I identified with the C-type predators I encountered and wanted what they seemed to want, just to connect and forget or discuss my life with someone. The type-C predators were more enjoyable people who even asked me to stay the night and have breakfast the next morning.

The third type of sexual predator I encountered was the D or (Dangerous)-type. They are called the D-type because even though they passed the pre-screening test, there was something particular about their behavior and language when I finally got to meet them; it gave me the feeling that I had put myself in a dangerous situation. For example, on one occasion I engaged in a dialogue and exchanged pics with one man who agreed to meet me at Splash, a gay bar.

Before leaving to meet the man I called Jason.

"I'm going to hook up with a guy I met on the Internet," I told Jason.

"You're crazy, don't you know that is dangerous?" he asked.

"Yeah, but I have to do it," I said.

"I'm meeting the guy at Splash, you want to come?" I asked.

"It's your date not mine," he said.

"Come, so you can see who I'm meeting," I said.

"What time will you be there?" he asked.

"I told him I'll meet him at 8:30. Let's meet at 8:15 across the street," I said.

"I'll see you there," Jason said as he hung up the phone.

Jason and I had worked out a system that we used in bars to indicate to one another if we wanted to get away from someone we had met. Jason was informed that I had agreed to hook up with the stranger at the back bar in Splash. We met as planned across the street from the club. Jason and I entered the club separately, so we did not give the impression that we were together.

When I arrived at the back bar, there were a few guys sitting and having drinks. Having exchanged pics and identifying information, I thought I knew what the man looked like and didn't see him at the bar. I arrived five minutes early and felt a little jilted when he did not show forty minutes later. After having a second soft drink I noticed a medium build man wearing Khakis and a light blue *Polo* shirt at the end of the bar who was there before I arrived. He approached me. His hair was dark brown and he had a goatee mustache.

"Hi my name is Bob," he said.

"I'm Michael," I said.

"Are you here alone?" he asked.

"Yes," I said.

"I've been watching you sitting here, you look lonely," he said.

After fifteen minutes and me telling him the story about being stood up, he began to talk to me about things that I talked about with the man online that I was originally scheduled to meet that night. I then realized that it was the same man I talked to online earlier and immediately discontinued the conversation as he tried to talk me into leaving with him. Jason passed by me and I swerved my drink around creating a whirlwind in the glass. This was the tornado code that was a sign to come take me away, like Dorothy was swept away in *The Wizard of Oz.*

The man had lied about his identity by sending me a pic of someone else he thought I'd be interested in and by his conversation it appeared he had something else in mind. He most likely had a collection of pictures that he sent depending on the descriptions others described to him.

On another occasion I met a D-type predator when I answered a personal ad. After talking to the person on the phone, I decided to meet him at Trinity Church. After a few moments into meeting him and leading him on to believe he gained my trust, the conversation became strange. He told me that he was looking for someone particular and that I fit his description as he did mine. The businessman was trying to persuade me to go with him to New Jersey and when I gave him the impression that I was going to go with him, he told me that we first had to stop and pick up a cutting device that was used to cut large boxes at a warehouse. No longer feeling safe I quickly decided to leave for home.

These four types of sexual predators were encountered online, in sex booths, porno theaters, clubs, bars, Central Park, newspaper ads and the Christopher Street pier. These interactions had to come to an end. Even with Lyle in my life, my curiosity and desire to know had to be satisfied. Once again I was at a crossroads where I had to make a decision to live a double life or not. Remembering my relationship with Cathy at Manhattanville, I decided living a double life is not worth it, so I remained faithful to Lyle. Having a relationship with him still did not resolve the desire to know and my struggle with it.

In my struggles I continued to relapse into mental illness with periods of dissociation and psychotic symptoms. On many occasions an all-seeing eye that held the knowledge of the universe appeared to me. My mind raced through the past and all the knowledge that I had stored in my brain, allowing me to see the future. The hallucinations I experienced led me to the bookshelves in my apartment and motivated me to pull books off the shelves one by one.

Stacking the books on the floor in separate piles, each pile represented an idea, and programmed knowledge in me that was trying to get out. The moments of illumination also led me to take apart my computer, but before taking it apart I journeyed through Internet dictionaries and encyclopedias on compact disks to compile information. I searched topics ranging from soul to electromagnetism. The subject areas were all connected in my mind, and I received the beauty of the universe, the one stanza that is God.

The moments of relapse also had a dark side. After the illumination phase ended, my mind went in the opposite direction. My mind was in total darkness. I developed a fear as I lay in bed with the covers over my head, having thoughts of vampires and a headless horseman. In my thoughts there were also servants of the Pope, kneeling down before him kissing his ring. Images of penises were jumping out at me in pictures of the Shroud of Turin.

After relapsing a final time I decided to write down my experiences in my journal. At 3:00 am one morning while away with Lyle I wrote:

> During the earlier episodes everyone was the dead living on earth. We were all fighting an evil force. Everyone in the house was like a vampire who could fly and change form as they left the house. They were all protecting me. I felt as if I was the last remaining soul on the earth and the

devil was trying to get my soul. This was my third episode as far as I can remember.

The first episode landed me in the hospital and the universal code was transcended to me. I had the power to see the truth. The next time it happened to me I could comprehend a beautiful God. I reached infinity in my mind and the transmission of God cannot be explained in words. I saw a light so powerful that I could only recognize it as the sun. God showed me the truth in a way that is as transparent as the breath of life. This beauty was not present around the second episode where death rose above me trying to take my life. I could see evil.

Through meditation on the Lord, God, Christ and medication, my mind stopped seeing the truth. The last episode left me with a strong feeling of what is to come. I was being fed insects to keep me alive. We were all in the middle of a holocaust and they were spraying the city to kill the mosquitoes that were carrying the West Nile Virus.

I stripped nude and wrapped myself as Christ was depicted in many movies. I blessed the house from evil and death that was to come. As I sat on the couch with my Bible in my hand and Ma's new translation, the world was about to begin again. It was Rosh Hashanah and I was chosen to hold the book of life open to allow the chosen souls into the book of life.

It was the night before that I could not sleep and was awakened during daybreak. It was then that I heard the horns blow twice. The sky was roaring with thunder. After the sound of the long trumpet, it was then that I saw the face of a lion. I was not afraid at the time. I screamed that God was coming to take us but he didn't. We were left for a reason.

I was enlightened that the knowledge that I was taught in the past was false wisdom and that I now know the truth. It was not until the next day that I realized we were chosen to help bring the souls through the book of life. I saw the burning bush as Ma once did and a lamb. As I held the book open, I could feel the power of the light flow into the book. I was shown the truth. I felt the power approaching the earth and go beyond it.

All that was going on inside of me continued to lead me to more searches. My research led me to the topic of the Illuminati and conspiracy theories. Later on I realized in therapy my searching on the outside was connected to what was going on inside my brain. My therapist wanted me to believe that I was possibly chemically unbalanced, but it was most likely the result of the abuse that I experienced as a child and the conspiracy I was involved in trying to keep the abuse a secret- in addition to all the events in my life of which I was ashamed.

Another topic that I researched was the Kundalini. Trying to understand what it was specifically that was happening to me on the inside was easily explained by the workings of the Kundalini. From the earliest memory I have of the abuse that began with the pressing on my lower back at the base of my spine, there was the power source in me awakened. This was my rationalization for a heightened awareness of what my body was doing.

My research also brought me to understand the all-seeing eye that was appearing before me. The understanding of my experiences with the all seeing eye led me to believe that, in God's view, I too was a fallen angel whose wings had been clipped. With the purging of my transgressions, my wounded soul could now heal. I believe that it is with the written word that the events of my life are documented and it is God's eye that has seen all there is, was, and is to come. I prayed as I awaited his final judgment.

In my wait, I went through stages in my hallucinations. My hallucinations propelled me to search in the hope of finding out what it all meant. The objects in my hallucinations were all signs and symbols. I researched signs and symbols on the Internet. My search led me to identify the objects in my hallucinations as Christian symbols. Little by little it was all making sense to me. Typing in Christian symbols led me to a site that showed symbols that appeared in my hallucinations. There was a Halo, Lion, Fire, Lamb, Book, and Eye.

As I concentrated on the symbols I began to scribble down in front of me one at a time the symbol and writing the first letter of each symbol before me. First I drew the halo, then the eye, then the lion, and stopped after drawing the lamb. My heart began to race when I realized I had spelled out the word **HELL**. The only two remaining symbols I did not write down were fire and book. My subconscious mind was telling me to put the two together; burn the book that I was writing. Like Claude-Adrien Helvetius' *De l'Esprit–Of the Island*–was to be just as atheistic, materialistic, sacrilegious, immoral and subversive.

Fighting my subconscious mind, it was telling me I was in hell and hell is where my soul was bound because of hurting Colin all those years ago. The fear that I developed for my past actions had prevented me from perpetuating the abuse as an adult. It was what Thomas Fawcett termed *The*

Symbolic Language of Religion that controlled my thoughts and behavior, so I did not act on any thoughts of sexual abuse. Suppressing thoughts may be viewed as a method for sexual predators to control their urges but it was not effective for me.

It is easier to acknowledge my thoughts and desires and to accept who I am and how I feel. Perhaps that is the difference between me, and someone who makes a career out of being a sexual predator. Self-realization helps stop the perpetuation of the cycle of abuse. My struggle with the desire to know about sexual predators and what I triumphed over almost becoming-that is a sexual predator- was put to rest one morning.

* * * *

I awoke from a peaceful night's rest to the shower running. Lyle was getting ready for work and it was now my turn for a shower. While I was in the shower I heard the phone ring. Drying off I heading back into the living room.

"Call home, your father was in a car accident," Lyle said.

I quickly called my apartment and Uriel answered.

"Uriel what happened?" I asked.

"Pa was crossing the street to buy Italian bread and a coffee while he was waiting for Melissa to get out of work. As he crossed the street a car attempted to beat the light and ran over him, " she said.

"Is he going to be alright?" I asked.

"He was hit so hard that his body flew in the air and his arm ripped from his body on the landing. He was brought to the triage center at Harlem Hospital, " she said.

I quickly hung up the phone and Lyle and I headed for the hospital to see my father. On the way to the hospital all I thought about was my relationship with my father and how we were just getting to communicate with one another. The idea of him no longer being alive circled over and over in my mind. I did not want to lose my father, not now. We were just getting to know one another.

When Lyle and I entered the hospital Ma, Benjamin and Melissa were in the waiting room. They directed me to the trauma room to see Pa. There he was lying on a board with his neck in a brace and his arm bandaged. The condition he was in was not as Uriel explained it to me. Pa looked very bad but I was prepared for worse. His arm was not ripped from his body but actually ripped open from the elbow to his wrist and the left side of his body was black and blue.

Like a code red the doctors surrounded Pa and began to examine him. As I stood there the doctors did not pull the curtains but pulled out a pairs of sheers and began cutting the clothing off his body. I just stood there in fear wanting to run but also wanting to be there for my father even though I felt he was never there for me growing up, after what I did to him while I was a child. My heart ached thinking this was the last time I was going to see him alive.

"Ouch!" Pa yelled as they cut his clothing off him and began poking and prodding.

"Can you feel this?" the doctor asked. He just looked up at me with tearful eyes unable to respond.

"Can you feel that?" she asked as she poked his stomach. He rolled his eyes and made a facial gesture indicating yes.

"Yes he can feel that," I yelled in the doctor's ear standing near me.

"How about that, does that hurt?" she asked. He indicated yes again.

"Yes he can feel that!" I yelled at her.

"Try to move your fingers," she said. Pa wiggled his fingers.

"Can you move your toes?" she asked. Pa moved his toes.

My father looked at me with tears in his eyes and slightly nodded his head in a yes gesture.

"Yes!" I said he could feel his toes moving. "He is moving his toes and his finger," I shouted.

Mentally, I was flashing back to my childhood and my lost relationship with my father as a result of my desire to know. As they continued to cut the clothing from my father they covered him up with a sheet. There I was standing before my father, as he lay there naked covered only by a sheet as I did that afternoon as a child. As they tried to turn my father over to check his spine the sheet fell over my father and landed on the side of the bed.

My father tried to catch the sheet with his injured arm as it fell-to cover himself- but it was too late. In a flash I finally saw what my father had between his legs and it was quickly covered over by the nurse as she pulled the sheet over him. After all those years the desire to know was satisfied and the negative Oedipal complex that I had subconsciously developed throughout my life was resolved. That event was the nail in the coffin that put to rest the lurking phantom of my desire to know. A feeling of freedom engulfed me, and softly as a whisper, I had the realization during that traumatic event that this angel had gotton its wings.

Epilogue

Jackson Avenue no longer looks like it did in the 1970's. Today P.S.21 and all of the tenement buildings are torn down and have been replaced with small townhouses. What was once a ghetto now appears to resemble suburbia with individual houses with gardens and tree lined blocks.

Ghettos are places for society's throwaways. The ghetto of the South Bronx was designed with rows of tenement apartment buildings with a cold architecture that appeared industrial, an echo of the industrial revolution. The apartments on Jackson Avenue also had a layout that matched its exterior. The rooms were laid out like the train tracks, hence the term railroad apartments.

To me the ghetto of the South Bronx resembled a rat maze and the apartments on Jackson Avenue were like Skinner boxes where human behavior was observed across the way by neighbors who peered in the windows to gather a body of knowledge. The residents watched their neighbors and reported their observations to a caseworker or Child Protective Services, another sector of the social service system.

It was this system that helped take my brother from my mother and place him in St. Joseph's with the intention to help, but instead created a sexual predator and unleashed him on us. It was St. Joseph's that programmed the sexual predator and allowed him to visit our apartment. It was like a mad scientist unleashing his experiment on the world while our neighbors functioned as data gatherers and passed on oral reports to the social service agencies so that they had the results of their experiment. Did their exist a working relationship between the State agencies and the Roman Catholic Church?

Families in our neighborhood practiced the act of confession when they reported their lives to social service workers and the Church. Both forces were working together in their attempts to improve family life, an act of bio-power.

This sounds like a conspiracy theory, but these connections help me understanding how the abuse came to be. It was a result of bio-power on a micro-level. The system did not fail because no one ever found out or reported the sexual abuse at the time it was happening. The system put in place works since this book is fulfilling the function some thirty-six years later.

I hope the system will use my experiences to improve itself. Douglas was released from prison in June 2003. Hopefully with the new sex offender registry laws, he will be registered and the next community he enters will be notified. As for me, it is the symbolic language of religion that keeps me in check.

About the Author

Bernard Amador was born in New York City in 1968 and is an Adjunct Instructor of Forensic Psychology at The College of New Rochelle's School of New Resources. He holds an M.A. in Forensic Psychology from Sage Graduate School, a B.A. in Forensic Psychology from the John Jay College of Criminal Justice, and a B.A. in Philosophy from Purchase College. He interned with the Domestic Violence and Child Abuse Bureau of the U.S. District Attorney's Office in White Plains, New York, at the Mental Health Association of New York, and worked as a Forensic Case Manager with a criminal justice agency. He lives in New York City and upstate New York.

Printed in the United States
22885LVS00001B/70